RSC

Mermaid Theatre

D0470196

Frank and Woji Gero and Playhouse Productions Ltd
present
the Swan Theatre production of

EVERY MAN IN HIS HUMOUR

by Ben Jonson

A programme/text with commentary by Simon Trussler

Contents

Swan Theatre Plays published by Methuen London
by arrangement with the Royal Shakespeare Company

methuen

Mermaid Theatre

The Royal Shakespeare Company (RSC), is the title under which the Royal Shakespeare Theatre, Stratford-upon-Avon, has operated since 1961. Now one of the best-known theatre companies in the world, the RSC builds on a long and distinguished history of theatre in Stratford-upon-Avon.

In essence, the aim of the Company is the same as that expressed in 1905 by Sir Frank Benson, then director of the Stratford theatre: 'to train a company, every member of which would be an essential part of a homogenous whole, consecrated to the practice of the dramatic arts and especially to the representation of the plays of Shakespeare'. The RSC is formed around a core of associate artists – actors, directors, designers and others – with the aim that their different skills should combine, over the years, to produce a distinctive approach to theatre, both classical and modern.

When, just a year after the granting, in 1925, of its Royal Charter, the theatre was almost completely destroyed by fire, a worldwide campaign was launched to build a new one. Productions moved to a local cinema until the new theatre, designed by Elisabeth Scott, was opened by the Prince of Wales on 23 April, 1932. Over the next thirty years, under the influence of directors such as Robert Atkins, Bridges-Adams, Iden Payne, Komisarjevsky, Sir Barry Jackson, Glen Byam Shaw and Anthony Quayle, the Shakespeare Memorial Theatre maintained a worldwide reputation.

In 1960, the newly appointed artistic director, Peter Hall, extended the re-named Royal Shakespeare Company's operations to include a London base at the Aldwych Theatre, and widened the Company's repertoire to include modern as well as classical work. Other innovations of the period which have shaped today's Company were the travelling Theatregoround and experimental work which included the Theatre of Cruelty season.

Under Trevor Nunn, who took over as artistic director in 1968, this experimental work in small performance spaces led, in 1974, to the opening of The Other Place, Stratford-upon-Avon. This was a rehearsal space converted into a theatre and in 1977 its London counterpart, The Warehouse, opened with a policy of presenting new British plays. In the same year the RSC played its first season in Newcastle upon Tyne – now an annual event. In 1978, the year in which Terry Hands joined Trevor Nunn as artistic director, the RSC also fulfilled an ambition to tour towns and villages with little or no access to live professional theatre.

In 1982, the RSC moved its London base to the Barbican Centre in the City of London, opening both the Barbican Theatre, specially built for the RSC by the generosity of the Corporation of the City of London, and The Pit, a small theatre converted like The Warehouse and The Other Place, from a rehearsal room.

Last season saw the opening of a new, fifth RSC theatre: the Swan Theatre in Stratford-upon-Avon. Built within the section of the shell of the original Shakespeare Memorial Theatre which escaped the 1926 fire, the Swan is a Jacobean-style playhouse staging the once hugely popular but now rarely-seen plays of Shakespeare's contemporaries during the period 1570-1750. This new dimension to the Royal Shakespeare Company's work has been made possible by the extremely generous gift of a benefactor, Frederick R. Koch. Many of the productions in this Mermaid Theatre season, presented by Frank and Woji Gero and Playhouse Productions Ltd, have transferred from that first, spectacularly successful, Swan season.

In early 1987 Terry Hands became sole Artistic Director and Chief Executive of the Company.

Throughout its history, the RSC has augmented its central operations with national and international tours, films, television programmes, commercial transfers and fringe activities. It has won over 200 national and international awards in its 25 years, including most recently the Queen's Award for Export – but despite box office figures which, it is thought, have no equal anywhere in the world, the costs of RSC activities cannot be recouped from ticket sales alone. We rely on assistance from the Arts Council of Great Britain, amounting to about 40% of our costs in any one year, from work in other media and, increasingly, from commercial sponsorship. To find out more about the RSC's activities and to make sure of priority booking for our productions, why not become a member of the Company's Mailing List. Details of how to apply can be found in the theatre foyer.

RSC

Mermaid Theatre

CAST IN ORDER OF APPEARANCE

Old Kno'well	**Stuart Richman**
Brainworm, *his servant*	**David Haig**
Master Stephen, *his nephew*	**Paul Greenwood**
Servant	**Roger Moss**
Ed Kno'well, *Old Kno'well's son*	**Simon Russell Beale**
Master Matthew	**Philip Franks**
Cob	**David Troughton**
Tib, *his wife*	**Susie Fairfax**
Captain Bobadill	**Pete Postlethwaite**
Thomas Kitely	**Henry Goodman**
Thomas Cash, *his clerk*	**Gary Love**
George Downright, *brother to Wellbred*	**Jeremy Pearce**
Dame Kitely	**Jane Galloway**
Bridget, *Kitely's sister*	**Jane Lancaster**
Wellbred, *brother to Downright*	**Nathaniel Parker**
Justice Clement	**Raymond Bowers**
Roger Formal, *his clerk*	**Mark Lindley**
Clement's servant	**Roger Moss**

Directed by	**John Caird**
Designed by	**Sue Blane**
Lighting by	**Wayne Dowdeswell**
Sound by	**John A Leonard** and **Mo Weinstock**
Fights by	**Malcolm Ranson**
Company voice work by	**Cicely Berry** and **Patsy Rodenburg**
Music Director	**Guy Woolfenden**
Design Assistant	**Jill Jowett**
Stage Management	**Richard Oriel**
Deputy Stage Manager	**Chantal Hauser**
Assistant Stage Manager	**Sara Myatt**

This performance is approximately 3 hours long including one interval of 20 minutes.

First performance of this RSC production, Swan Theatre, Stratford-upon-Avon, 15 May 1986
Mermaid Theatre, London 8 April 1987

Please do not smoke or use cameras or tape recorders in the auditorium. And please remember that noise such as whispering, coughing, rustling programmes and the bleeping of digital watches can be distracting to performers and also spoils the performance for other members of the audience.

Arts Council Funded

Biographies

SIMON RUSSELL BEALE *Ed Kno'well*
Theatre: Theobald Maske in *Die Hose, Points of Departure*, Sandra in *Sandra/Manon, The Death of Elias Sawney* (Traverse Theatre, Edinburgh), Osric in *Hamlet* (Lyceum, Edinburgh). *Look to the Rainbow* (London), The Ward in *Women Beware Women* (Royal Court).
RSC: Young Shepherd in *The Winter's Tale*, Ed Kno'well in *Every Man in His Humour*, Oliver in *The Art of Success*, Fawcett in *The Fair Maid of the West*.

SUE BLANE *Designer*
Theatre: Numerous designs for theatre including *Galileo, Jungle Of The Cities, Loot, The Government Inspector, Mother Goose, Dick Whittington, Puss In Boots, Cinderella, Pymalion, Fears & Miseries Of The Third Reich, The Good Humoured Ladies* (Citizens' Theatre), *Katya Kabanova, Ivan Susanin, The Two Widows, La Vestale* (Wexford Festival Opera-Eire), *The Poisoned Kiss* (London Opera Centre), *Dialogue Of The Carmelites* (RNCM), *The Bartered Bride, The Golden Cockerel, Hansel And Gretel, The Two Widows* (Scottish Opera), *The Milk Train Doesn't Stop Here Any More, Babes In The Wood, Jack And The Beanstalk, Hello Hollywood Hello, Bus Stop, Irma La Douce, Guys And Dolls, Cabaret, Pygmalion, The Merchant of Venice, Blythe Spirit, Otherwise Engaged, Side by Side by Sondheim, Summer* (Watford Palace Theatre), costumes for *The Rocky Horror Show* (Theatre Upstairs, Royal Court, Kings Road Theatre, US, Australia, Oslo), costumes for *Tooth Of Crime, T.Zee And The Lost Race, A Short Sharp Shock* (Royal Court Theatre), *City Sugar*, (Michael White Ltd), *Twisted Cues And Elliptical Balls* (Arts Theatre), *Design For Living* (Northcott Theatre), *Whose Life Is It Anyway?* (Churchill Theatre, Bromley), *The Worlds* (Half Moon), costumes for *Guys And Dolls* (NT), *A Midsummer Night's Dream, Mother Courage* (South Australia Theatre Company), *The Marriage of Figaro* (Gelsinkirchen), *The Gambler* (ENO), *Die Fledermaus* (Opera North), *Abbacadbra* (Lyric, Hammersmith), *Way Of The World* (Greenwich), *Carousel* (Royal Exchange), *Corpse* (Apollo), *Guys And Dolls* (tour & Prince Of Wales Theatre), *Porgy And Bess* (Glyndebourne), *The Mikado* (ENO), *High Society* (Haymarket, Leicester).
RSC: *Everyman In His Humour*.
Films: Includes costumes for *The Rocky Horrow Show, Shock Treatment, The Draughtsman's Contract, Lady Jane, Absolute Beginners*.

RAYMOND BOWERS *Justice Clement*
Theatre: includes Player King in *Rosencrantz and Guildenstern Are Dead*, Leonato in *Much Ado About Nothing*, Enobarbus in *Antony and Cleopatra* (Repertory), *Male of the Species, Charley's Aunt* (London).
RSC: Lord/Pedant in *The Taming of the Shrew*, Jodelet in *Cyrano de Bergerac* (also USA), Archbishop Monselet in *Red Noses*, Antigonus in *The Winter's Tale*, Justice Clement in *Every Man in His Humour*, Bushy/Gardener in *Richard II*.
Television: *The Citadel, Are You Being Served?, Cyrano de Bergerac*.
Film: *Callan, Are You Being Served?*

JOHN CAIRD *Director*
Theatre: *Song And Dance* (London), *As You Like It* (Stadsteaten, Stockholm).
RSC: Associate Director of the RSC. *The Dance of Death, Savage Amusement, The Merry Wives of Windsor, Look Out . . . Here Comes Trouble!, The Caucasian Chalk Circle, Naked Robots, Nicholas Nickleby* (London and New York), *The Twin Rivals, Our Friends in the North, Peter Pan, Twelfth Night, Romeo and Juliet, The Merchant of Venice, Red Star, Philistines, Les Misérables* (London and New York), *Everyman in His Humour, Misalliance*.
Television: *As You Like It* (Sweden).

WAYNE DOWDESWELL *Lighting*
Theatre; *The Fantasticks, Salad Days*, Verdi's *Macbeth, Nabucco* and *Aida*, Mozart's *Cosi Fan Tutte, Don Giovanni* (Sheffield University Theatre), *No More Sitting On The Old School Bench, Painted Veg and Parkinson, Fanshen, Hunchback of Notre Dame* (Manchester Contact Theatre).
RSC: Joined the RSC in 1978. Worked at TOP as Deputy Electrician and the Electrician. TOP productions include *Money, Golden Girls, Desert Air, Today, The Dillen, Mary After the Queen, The Quest*. Currently Resident Lighting Designer at the Swan Theatre where his productions include *The Two Noble Kinsmen, Every Man in His Humour, The Rover* and *The Fair Maid of the West*.

SUSIE FAIRFAX *Tib*
Theatre: Seasons at Plymouth, Coventry. Toine in *Piaf*, Thelma Sparrow in *Birdbath*, Mrs Dai Bread/Rosie Probert in *Under Milkwood*, Liddy Smallbury in *Far from the Madding Crowd*, Nerissa in *The Merchant of Venice, Pygmalion, Equus, Devonshire Cream* (Repertory). The Woman in *After Liverpool* (Soho Poly). *Roots, The Devil's Disciple, The Royal Pardon* (UK tours).
RSC: Lady in *The Winter's Tale*, Tib in *Every Man in His Humour*, Valeria in *The Rover*.
Television: *Winter Sunshine, Partners in Crime, Agatha Christie, My Cousin Rachel, Reilly-Ace of Spires, Fame is the Spur, Stalky and Co, Bognor, God Speed Co-operation, Nanny, Adelaide Bartlett-A Question of Guilt*.
Film: *Winter Flight, Tarka the Otter*.

PHILIP FRANKS *Master Matthew*
Theatre: Seasons at Edinburgh, Oxford, Coventry. Title role in *Edward II*, Raskolnikov in *Crime and Punishment*, Romeo in *Romeo and Juliet*, title role in *Billy Budd*, Kaa the Python in *The Jungle Book*, Ariel in *The Tempest*, Octavius Caesar in *Antony and Cleopatra* (Chichester Festival Theatre). Bob/Henry in *Heroes* (New End Theatre, London). Bassanio in *The Merchant of Venice* (UK tour).
RSC: Lysander in *A Midsummer Night's Dream*, Bassianus in *Titus Andronicus*, Outlaw in *The Two Gentlemen of Verona*, Bertram in *All's Well That Ends Well*, Florizel in *The Winter's Tale*, John Darling in *Peter Pan*, Gloucester/Morton/Shadow in *Henry IV*, Matthew in *Every Man in His Humour*, Henry Fielding in *The Art of Success*, Gaston in *Worlds*

Apart. Directed *Come Unto These Yellow Sands* (RSC Festival).
Television: *Bleak House, To Serve Them All My Days, The Inner Eye.*
Design: *Revelations* (Chichester), *Erismena* (Midsummer Opera).
Writing: *A Warning To the Curious* (Chichester).

JANE GALLOWAY *Dame Kitely*
Theatre: Seasons at Worcester, Bristol, Birmingham. Hippolyta in *A Midsummer Night's Dream*, Diana in *All's Well That Ends Well*, Jessica in *The Merchant of Venice*, Jane in *One For the Road*, Lizzie in *Piggy Back Riders*. Audrey in *As You Like It* (Birmingham). Kathy in *Care* (Royal Court), Anna Laub in *Silver Foxes Trilogy* (Gate Theatre, London). Charlotte Lucas in *Pride and Prejudice* (UK tour), *Village Wooing* (Copenhagen).
RSC: *The Quest,* Dame Kitely in *Every Man in His Humour*, Mary in *Pure Silence*, Deirdre in *A Piece for the Palate* (RSC Festival).
Television: *Bull Week, The Gentle Touch, The Borgias, Eh Brian it's a Whopper.*
Film: *The Red Monarch.*
Radio: *The Archers,* Several Radio plays most recently *The White Peacock.*

HENRY GOODMAN *Thomas Kitely*
Theatre: Krogstad in *A Doll's House*, Vladimir in *Waiting for Godot*, Christoforou in *Private Ear/Public Eye*, Voltaire/Dr Pangloss in *Candide*, Missionary in *The Fantastical History of a Useless Man*, Sidney in *Absurd Person Singular*, Lopakhin in *The Cherry Orchard*, title role in *Tartuffe*, Shylock in *The Merchant of Venice*, Bosola in *The Duchess of Malfi*, Dr Ranz in *What the Butler Saw*, Gregor Samsa in *Metamorphosis*, Klyestakov in *The Government Inspector*, Dad in *The Guinea Fowl*, Home Secretary in *Claw*, title role in *Groucho Marx*, Captain Hook in *Peter Pan*, Henry Hackamore in *Seduced*, Steve/Les in *Decadence*, Malcolm in *Bedroom Farce* (Repertory).
RSC: Harry in *The Time of Your Life*, Lovell/Archbishop of Canterbury in *Henry VIII*, Voltore in *Volpone*, Dromio of Ephesus in *The Comedy of Errors*, Azhog/Stalin in *Red Star*, Prince Henri de Conde in *The Devils*, Grandpré/le Fer in *Henry V*, Corporal/Second Man in *War Plays*, Paulina's Steward/Time in *The Winter's Tale*, Thomas Kitely in *Every Man in His Humour*, Fernando in *Worlds Apart*. Directed *Close Encounters of the Swan Kind – Marlowe and Jonson* and *Ogun Abibiman* by *Wole Soyinka* (RSC Festival).
Television: *The Golden Bowl, Max Beerbohm, Chicken Run, Mickey Kannis Caught My Eye, Good News.*
Directing: Includes *The Fall and Redemption of Man, Rooted, I'm Ready For You Miss Jones, Lovers, Neighbours, Sweet Bird of Youth, Hail Wedded Love, Fanshen, Bye Bye Blues, Hello Howzit, Tests, Doggs Our Pet, The Parents, Agamemnon, People's Space Roadshow.* Artistic Director for People's Space Theatre, Cape Town, 1980. *The Provok'd Wife, Berlin Kabarett* (Guildhall School of Music and Drama).
Radio: Numerous broadcasts, most recently *The Scarlet Pimpernel, Pros and Cons, The Cherry Orchard, Voyage of Osiris.*

PAUL GREENWOOD *Master Stephen*
Theatre: Seasons at Chesterfield, Bromley, Harrogate, Birmingham, Windsor, Coventry. Romeo in *Romeo and Juliet*, Prince Hal in *Henry IV*, Oberon/Thesus in *A Midsummer Night's Dream*, Christy Mahon in *Playboy of the Western World*, Norman in *The Norman Conquests*, Chris in *All My Sons*, Fancourt Babberly in *Charley's Aunt*, Dame in *Jack in the Beanstalk*, Dame in *Mother Goose*, Ugly Sister in *Cinderella*, Dame in *Jack the Giant Killer*, title role in *Peer Gynt* (Repertory), *Twelfth Night*, *Inadmissable Evidence* (Royal Court), *June Evening, Absurd Person Singular, Funny Peculiar, The Good Doctor, Goosepimples* (UK tours).
RSC: *Once in a Lifetime, Piaf,* Tom in *The Time of Your Life*, Cromwell in *Henry VIII*, Antipholus of Syracuse in *The Comedy of Errors*, Tassell in *The Happiest Days of Your Life*, Polixenes in *The Winter's Tale*, Master Stephen in *Every Man in His Humour*, Lysander in *A Midsummer Night's Dream*, Goodlack in *The Fair Maid of the West*.
Television: *Rosie, Heartland, Coronation Street, Lulu Show, No Trams to Lime Street, A Day Out, Captain Zep, The Growing Pains of Adrian Mole.*
Teaching: Teaches at National Film School and Actors' Centre.
Writing: Wrote and sang signature tune for Rosie.

DAVID HAIG *Brainworm*
Theatre: Seasons at Birmingham, Oxford, Cambridge, Windsor, Stoke. Launcelot Gobbo in *The Merchant of Venice*, Norman in *And A Nightingale Sang* (Repertory). Maurice Haig-wood in *Tom and Viv* (also New York), Dave in *Care*, Sam in *The Arbor*, Young Writers' Festival (all Royal Court).
RSC: Dudley Bostwick in *The Time of Your Life*, Corvino in *Volpone*, Brainworm in *Every Man in His Humour*, Quince in *A Midsummer Night's Dream*, Joaquin in *Worlds Apart*.
Television: *Chessgame, Flame to the Phoenix, Diamonds, Moon Stallion, Dr Who, Blake's Seven.*
Film: *Horrors from Outer Space.*
Radio: *Howard's End, A Day Out, Men.*

JANE LANCASTER *Bridget*
Theatre: *Betty and the Bombshells* (Edinburgh Festival 1985), Christine Daaé in *Phantom of the Opera* (Contact Theatre Manchester 1985), Mrs Rafi in *The Sea* (Manchester Independent Theatre Co), Work with Merseyside Young Peoples' Theatre.
RSC: Fairy in *A Midsummer Night's Dream*, Lady/Singer in *Richard II*, Bridget in *Every Man in His Humour*, Sue Hammond in *Country Dancing; Simply Sondheim, The Silver King* (RSC Festival).
Television: *Albion Market.*

MARK LINDLEY *Roger Formal*
Theatre: Seasons at Victoria Theatre, Stoke-on-Trent and Century Theatre, Keswick. Polonius in *Hamlet*, Harvey in *Seasons Greetings*, Aslaksen in *Enemy of the People*, Monsieur Richard in *Phantom of the Opera*, (Repertory). Reeve in *Canterbury Tales*, Merriman in *The Importance of Being Earnest* (Century Theatre UK tours).

RSC: Officer in *The Winter's Tale*, Roger Formal in *Every Man in His Humour*, York's Servant/Murderer in *Richard II*, Young Siward in *Macbeth*.
Television: *Coronation Street, Emmerdale Farm.*

GARY LOVE *Thomas Cash*
Theatre: Tulsa in *Gypsy* (Ipswich), Alan Strang in *Equus*, Nicely Nicely Johnson in *Guys and Dolls*, Dustin in *Starlight Express*, Young Kevin in *Tommy* (London), One of the Lads in *Oliver* (London and UK tour).
RSC: Pastoral Servant in *The Winter's Tale*, Thomas Cash in *Every Man in His Humour*, Drawer/Sailor/Spanish Prisoner in *The Fair Maid of the West*.
Television: *Options, The Cage, Missing from Home, Grange Hill, Starting Out.*

ROGER MOSS *Servant/Clement's Servant*
Theatre: Troilus in *Troilus and Cressida*, Dumaine in *Love's Labour's Lost*, Dr Wicksteed in *Habeas Corpus* (OUDS). Romeo in *Romeo and Juliet*, Sir Andrew Aguecheek in *Twelfth Night*, Sir Thomas More in *A Man for All Seasons* (National Youth Theatre), Job in *Job: The Musical* (Wooden O), Malcolm in *Macbeth* (UK tour).
RSC: Pastoral Servant in *The Winter's Tale*, Postboy/Gasper in *Every Man in His Humour*, Footman/Fairy in *A Midsummer Night's Dream*, Groom in *Richard II*. Oberon in *Come Unto These Yellow Sands*, Racks in *Class Enemy* (RSC Festival).

NATHANIEL PARKER *Wellbred*
Theatre: Season at Theatr Clwyd, Mold. Captain Brazen in *The Recruiting Officer*, Lusby in *Claw* (Repertory). Tybalt in *Romeo and Juliet* (Young Vic), title role in *Macbeth* (National Youth Theatre). LAMDA and National Youth Theatre tours to Europe.
RSC: Florizel in *The Winter's Tale*, Wellbred in *Every Man in His Humour*, Don Pedro in *The Rover*, Hotspur in *Richard II*. Oliver in *The Kiss* (RSC Festival).

JEREMY PEARCE *George Downright*
Theatre: Seasons at Nottingham Playhouse, Newcastle, Ipswich, Pitlochry, Chester, Westcliff, Colchester, Musselburgh. Mickey in *Blood Brothers*, The Superintendent in *Accidental Death of an Anarchist*, Bill Sykes in *Oliver*, Haddock in *No More Sitting On The Old School Bench* (Repertory). Dull in *Love's Labour's Lost* (Playhouse, Nottingham), Graham in *Time and Time Again* (Brunton, Edinburgh), Father Mullarkey in *Once A Catholic* (Gateway, Chester). Big Lonnie in *Midnight* (Almost Free). Dogberry in *Much Ado About Nothing* (Shakespeare Festival, Bourges).
RSC: *Antony and Cleopatra* (TV), Downright in *Every Man in His Humour*, Menendez in *Worlds Apart*, Menteith in *Macbeth*, (RSC Festival) *Lynchville* and *Silver King*.
Television: *Spy Trap, Thriller, The Gentle Touch, The Bill, Worzel Gummidge, The Awful Mr Goodall, Churchill's People.*
Film: *The Hiding Place, O Lucky Man, Wildcats of St Trinians, Jacko.*

PETE POSTLETHWAITE *Captain Bobadill*
Theatre: Seasons at Bristol and Liverpool. O'Rourke in *The Bofors Gun*, title role in Brecht's *Coriolanus, A View From the Bridge, Titus Andronicus, Destiny*, Nathan Detroit in *Guys and Dolls* (Repertory). Antonio in *The Duchess of Malfi* (Royal Exchange Manchester and Round House). *Funny Peculiar, Breezeblock Park* (London), *Magnificence, Cromwell, Flying Blind* (Royal Court), *Having a Ball, Favourite Nights* (Lyric Hammersmith).
RSC: Macduff in *Macbeth*, Cornwall in *King Lear*, Soldier in *Lear*, Grumio in *The Taming of the Shrew*, Walt in *The Body*, Ragueneau in *Cyrano de Bergerac*, Hastings in *Richard III*, Exeter in *Henry V*, Brodin in *Red Noses*, Captain Bobadill in *Every Man in His Humour*, Bottom in *A Midsummer Night's Dream*, Roughman in *The Fair Maid of the West*.
Television: *Play for Today - The Muscle Market, Crown Court, Coronation Street, Mitch, Minder.*
Film: *A Private Function.*
Directing: *Funny Peculiar, One Flew Over the Cuckoo's Nest* (Bristol).

MALCOLM RANSON *Fight Director*
Theatre: Has directed fights in Germany, Norway, Switzerland and Ireland. *The Three Musketeers, The Duchess of Malfi, Hamlet, Entertaining Mr Sloane, As You Like It, Cymbeline* (Royal Exchange, Manchester), *Hamlet* (Royal Court), *The Prisoner of Zenda* (Contact Theatre Company), *The Mayor of Zalamea, The Spanish Tragedy, Lorenzaccio, Coriolanus, Up For None, The Critic, Hamlet* (NT). *The Scarlet Pimpernel* (Chichester and West End), *This Story of Yours* (Hampstead), *Carmen Jones, Tom Jones, Twelfth Night* (Crucible Sheffield).
RSC: *Henry IV Parts 1 and 2, The Knight of the Burning Pestle, The Twin Rivals, Macbeth, Henry IV, King Lear*, Bond's *Lear, Peter Pan, Julius Caesar, Twelfth Night, A Midsummer Night's Dream, Romeo and Juliet, Richard III, Red Star, Hamlet, Troilus and Cressida, Les Liaisons Dangereuses* (London & New York), *Les Misérables* (London & New York), *Romeo and Juliet, Richard II, The Fair Maid of the West, Macbeth.*
Television: *Henry VI Parts 1, 2 and 3, Richard III, The Critic, Vorpal Blade, Coriolanus, By the Sword Divided, Black Adder, Submariners, Titus Andronicus, Casualty.*
Directing: Co-director, with John Blackmore, and fight director on *Treasure Island* (Newcastle Playhouse), co-director, with Michael Bogdanov, and fight director on *The Sound of Music* (Tokyo).

STUART RICHMAN *Old Kno'well*
Theatre: Founder member of Liverpool Everyman Theatre: Tesman in *Hedda Gabler*, Aston in *The Caretaker*, Becket in *Murder in the Cathedral*, Vanya in *Uncle Vanya*, Con Melody in *Touch of a Poet*. Mike in *Ruffian on the Stair*, Arvide Abernathy in *Guys and Dolls*, Antigonus in *The Winter's Tale* (Chester), Aslakson in *An Enemy of the People* (Lancaster), Joseph in *Coventry Mystery Plays* (Coventry Cathedral), Antrobus in *Skin of our Teeth* (Leeds Playhouse), Macduff in *Macbeth* (Sheffield), Adam in *As You Like It* (Stoke), Mr Proudfoot in *Class K*, Ruckley in *One Flew Over the Cuckoo's Nest* (Royal Exchange Manchester and UK tour). Guildenstern in Marowitz' *Hamlet* (London, Italy), Marowitz' *Faustus* (Frankfurt), *The Recruiting Officer*, one man play *The Man Himself* (Oxford Playhouse tour of UK and Hong Kong).
RSC: *The Devils, Troilus and Cressida, Curtmantle* (1962), Ted Rogers in *Country Dancing*.
Television: *Z Cars, The Doctors, The Gathering Seed, Arthur Ransome, Gaskin, Losers Weepers, Encounter with a Mad Man, Flame to the Phoenix, Book-Tower, The Practice, The Road to 1984, Bulman, Public Eye, Brookside, Lost Empires, Victorian Values.*
Film: *Reds, The Dresser.*
Radio: many plays for BBC Radio, Radio Merseyside, Radio City, Piccadilly Radio.

Poetry Readings, Theatre in Education.

DAVID TROUGHTON *Cob*
Theatre: Seasons at Arts Theatre and Leeds Playhouse. Knocker White in *The Wedding Feast, No More Sitting on the Old School Bench* (Leeds), Evans in *Terra Nova* (Watford), *The Case of the Frightened Lady* (Bromley). Martin in *Fool for Love*, Peter in *Don Juan, Serjeant Musgraves's Dance* (NT). Hal in *Loot* (Royal Court).
RSC: Ross in *Macbeth*, Conrad in *Much Ado About Nothing*, Aslak in *Peer Gynt*, Bouton in *Molière*, Clown in Antony and Cleopatra, Sebastian in *The Roaring Girl*, Cob in *Every Man in His Humour*, Blunt in *The Rover*, Porter in *Macbeth*.
Television: Includes *David Copperfield, Chips with Everything, Our Mutual Friend, The Norman Conquests, Wings, Man of Destiny, Hi-De-Hi, Sorry, Angels, A Very Peculiar Practice.*
Film: *Dance With A Stranger, The Chain.*
Radio: *Psmith.*

FRANK and WOJI GERO *Producers*
Frank and Woji Gero met as actors at the Woodstock Playhouse, Illinois in January, 1951 and married the same year. Frank earned a BA in Drama from Loyola University and Woji from Mundelein College in Chicago before moving East. Both have been involved in all aspects of theatre on over 200 productions.

They have produced 15 plays in New York, including *Are You Now or Have You Ever Been, Extremities* and *The Miss Firecracker Contest. On Golden Pond, Key Exchange,* and *Eric Bogozian Funhouse* were co-produced with Frederick M. Zollo.

On a trip to London in 1985 for the opening of *Extremities*, they saw a performance of Stephen Poliakoff's *Breaking the Silence* at the RSC's Pit Theatre and later presented it at the Mermaid Theatre. This started a successful working relationship with the RSC and was soon followed by Pam Gems' *Camille* and then by the hugely successful *Les Liaisons Dangereuses.*

Frank and Woji Gero have four sons: Jonathan and Jason, actors, Christopher, a film maker, and Mark, a sculptor married to Liza Minnelli.

PLAYHOUSE PRODUCTIONS LTD *Producers*
Playhouse Productions was formed in 1986 in order to refurbish the Playhouse Theatre in Northumberland Avenue. The theatre will open in the summer of this year, meaning that London will regain a West End theatre, which has not staged a live show for 35 years.

Playhouse Productions has in the past year been proud to be associated with *The Miss Firecracker Contest, Les Liaisons Dangereuses,* and *Spin of the Wheel* (co-production with Michael White).

RSC

Royal Shakespeare Company

Stratford-upon-Avon Box Office (0789) 295623

ROYAL SHAKESPEARE THEATRE	SWAN THEATRE	THE OTHER PLACE

ROYAL SHAKESPEARE THEATRE

Julius Caesar
by William Shakespeare
directed by Terry Hands

The Merchant of Venice
by William Shakespeare
directed by Bill Alexander

Twelfth Night
by William Shakespeare
directed by Bill Alexander

The Taming of the Shrew
by William Shakespeare
directed by Jonathan Miller

Measure for Measure
by William Shakespeare
directed by Nicholas Hytner

SWAN THEATRE

Hyde Park
by James Shirley
directed by Barry Kyle

Titus Andronicus
by William Shakespeare
directed by Deborah Warner

The Jew of Malta
by Christopher Marlowe
directed by Barry Kyle

The Revenger's Tragedy
by Cyril Tourneur
directed by Di Trevis

The New Inn
by Ben Jonson, directed by John Caird

THE OTHER PLACE

Fashion
by Doug Lucie
directed by Nick Hamm
commissioned and presented
by arrangement with Michael Codron

Temptation
by Havel translated by George Theiner
directed by Roger Michell

Indigo
by Heidi Thomas
directed by Sarah Pia Anderson

A Question of Geography
by John Berger and Nella Bielski
directed by John Caird

Cymbeline
by William Shakespeare
directed by Bill Alexander

London Box Office (01) 628 8795

BARBICAN THEATRE

Macbeth
by William Shakespeare
directed by Adrian Noble

Romeo and Juliet
by William Shakespeare
directed by Michael Bogdanov

Richard II
by William Shakespeare
directed by Barry Kyle

THE PIT

Country Dancing
by Nigel Williams
directed by Bill Alexander

Worlds Apart
by Jose Triana, adapted by Peter Whelan
directed by Nick Hamm

Sarcophagus
by Vladimir Gubaryev
Translated by Michael Glenny
directed by Jude Kelly

MERMAID THEATRE

The Fair Maid Of The West
by Thomas Heywood
directed by Trevor Nunn

Every Man In His Humour
by Ben Jonson
directed by John Caird

The Two Noble Kinsmen
by William Shakespeare and John Fletcher
directed by Barry Kyle

RSC in the West End

PALACE THEATRE
Box Office (01) 437 6834/8327
Les Miserables
The Victor Hugo musical

AMBASSADORS THEATRE
Box Office (01) 836 6111
Les Liaisons Dangereuses
by Christopher Hampton

THE OLD VIC
Box Office (01) 928 7616
Kiss Me Kate
Cole Porter's musical from 8 May

RSC

Mermaid Theatre

Royal Shakespeare Company
Incorporated under Royal Charter as the
Royal Shakespeare Theatre
Patron Her Majesty the Queen
President Sir Kenneth Cork
Chairman of the Council Geoffrey A Cass
Vice Chairman Dennis L Flower
Artistic Director Terry Hands
Direction Peggy Ashcroft John Barton Peter Brook
Terry Hands Trevor Nunn
Technical Services Administrator John Bradley
General Manager David Brierley
Publicity Controller Peter Harlock
Production Controller James Langley
Planning Controller Tim Leggatt
Senior Administrator Genista McIntosh
Barbican Administrator James Sargant
Financial Controller William Wilkinson

Artistic Director Mermaid Theatre Ron Daniels

Casting Siobhan Bracke
Publicity Stephen Browning
Press Caro Newling (01-628 3351)
Marketing Alison Shakspeare
Company Manager Trevor Williamson

For Frank & Woji Gero and Playhouse Productions Ltd
General Manager Andrew Treagus Associates (01-734 4274)
Assistant to the Producers Gail Berryman
Production Manager Forbes Nelson

For Gomba Holdings (UK) Ltd
Administrator Tim O'Regan

Production Credits for Every Man in His Humour
Scenery, properties, costumes and wigs made and painted in
RST Workshops, Stratford-upon-Avon. Additional costumes by
Fran Bristow, Sue Wyatt. Production photographs by Donald
Cooper. Buns supplied by Peter Stratton. Stage alterations by
John Collins Construction Ltd and the Mermaid Theatre
Workshop. RSC programme compiled by Jo Denbury.

For the Mermaid Theatre
General Manager Barbara Penney
Technical Manager Forbes Nelson
Conference and Exhibition Manager Alison Heys
House Manager Christopher Playford
Box Office Manager Sarah Eastwood (01 236 5568)
Chief Electrician Lorraine Richards
Master Carpenter Patrick Ayling
Wardrobe Maintenance Louise DeVille Morel
Wig Maintenance Sarah Phillips & Co
Accounts Stuart Wise
Catering Manager Barry Myers

Food and Drink
Bridge Bar
A traditionally stocked bar (including draught beers) open for
lunch 12-3pm, before and after performances from 5pm.
Dockyard Wine Bar
Open before show from 5pm – interesting wine list and wide
selection of bottled beers.
Food Bar
Open for lunch and pre-performance (times as above), serving
home-made soups, house specialities and fruit salad; and a wide
range of salads and gateaux. Patrons wishing to eat after the
performance please place your order before the show.

Mermaid Theatre Art Gallery 1987/88

16 March – 27 April	**Tim Harris**
27 April – 8 June	**Ross Scrivener**
8 June – 20 July	**Paulette Collier**
20 July – 31 August	**Colin Darke**
31 August – 23 November	**Gordon Aldred**
23 November – 4 January 1988	**Jackie Lancaster**

For further information about these exhibitions, please contact
Alison Heys on 01-236 9521.

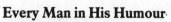

Every Man in His Humour

left:
Pete Postlethwaite: CAPTAIN BOBADILL,
Paul Greenwood: MASTER STEPHEN,
Roger Moss: CLEMENT'S SERVANT,
Simon Russell Beale: ED KNO'WELL

below:
Gary Love: THOMAS CASH
Henry Goodman: THOMAS KITELY

opposite page top left:
David Troughton: COB
top right:
Pete Postlethwaite: CAPTAIN BOBADILL,
Philip Franks: MASTER MATTHEW
bottom:
Simon Russell Beale: ED KNO'WELL
Paul Greenwood: MASTER STEPHEN
David Haig: BRAINWORM

Director's Note; 'An Image of the Times'

. . . deeds and language, such as men do use,
And persons such as Comedy would choose,
When she would show an Image of the Times . . .

Ben Jonson makes it very clear in the prologue to the folio edition of 1616 what he wants *Every Man in His Humour* to be, to his reader and to his audience. How odd then that 18 years earlier in 1598 when the play was first performed (quarto version) he had bowed to the convention of the times and set it in Florence with a cast of Italian characters. It is not known precisely when he rewrote the play but the later folio version is the work of a much more mature and confident playwright who, having the courage of his convictions, has made all the characters unmistakably English and has set the play firmly where it belongs, in London.

Apart from the obvious rightness of the English setting, the later folio is superior to the earlier quarto in nearly every respect. The poetry is richer, the rhythm of the writing more assured and the characters more sharply defined. I have, however, pillaged the quarto for some significant changes. In 1606 an act was passed in Parliament 'For the preventing and avoyding of the greate Abuse of the Holy Name of God in Stageplayes . . .', threatening that if 'any person or persones doe or shall in any Stage play . . . jestingly or prophanely speake or use the Holy Name of God or of Jesus Christ, or of the Holy Ghoste or of the Trinitie . . . (such person or persones) shall forfeit for everie such Offence by hym or them committed Tenne Pounds . . .'

At ten pounds an oath, a production of the quarto version of *Every Man in His Humour* would have bankrupted Jonson overnight! His attempts to deblasphemise his earlier play produced some inspired results, particularly in the dialogue of Captain Bobadill. We are thus indebted to the censor for some of the most inventive oaths in the English language. Elsewhere, however, the text suffers from the coy alternatives to profanity typical of this period, and where I have felt that the original oaths take us nearer to Jonson's real, earthy and observed intention, they have been retained. At times the folio text is incomprehensible to modern ears, either through topical reference or linguistic obscurity, and where a cut would be inappropriate, I have returned to the quarto for clarity's sake.

The only major departure from the folio is in the last scene, where I have conflated the two texts to a considerable degree. The end of the play in the folio version is wrapped up all too neatly, and with too many unanswered questions. I have retained from the quarto Edward Kno'well's wonderful speech on the nature of true poetry, without which his character, his father's, and their relationship to each other would remain sadly unresolved. For the same reason I have included the fraternal reconciliation of Wellbred and Downright, and the matrimonial one of Kitely and his wife.

I have cut Kitely's unsatisfactory and conventional poem about horns, and replaced it with Jonson's own remarkable poem 'Against Iealousie', first published as part of his *Underwoods* in 1640.

Much of the detailed editing work and most of the cutting has been done in rehearsal, and I am greatly indebted to my cast of actors for their considerable editorial skills.

John Caird
Stratford, April 1986

Commentary
compiled by Simon Trussler

Stage History

Until the mid-nineteenth century, *Every Man in His Humour* was one of Ben Jonson's most popular plays. There is even an apocryphal tradition that Shakespeare personally recommended this very early work by an almost unknown playwright to his company. Certainly, it was the Lord Chamberlain's Men who gave the play its first performance in 1598, probably around mid-September, at a time when they are thought to have been playing at the Curtain Theatre in Shoreditch, between the recent closure of the nearby Theatre and the opening of the new Globe on the Bankside. And Shakespeare himself is listed first among the principal players in the folio edition of the play, perhaps taking the part of Old Kno'well, with the celebrated comic actors Will Kempe and Will Slye also among the cast.

Our knowledge of the day-to-day repertory of the Elizabethan and Jacobean theatres is sketchy, but *Every Man in His Humour* seems to have enjoyed continuing popularity among the plays of the King's Men (as Shakespeare's company were known after 1603). A performance at court is recorded in 1605, and another as late as 1631 – a season for which, exceptionally, a complete record has been preserved. And the choice of the play by the Master of the Revels for one of the 'benefit performances' granted to him in 1628 suggests that this canny official knew it to be still good box-office.

During the Restoration and early eighteenth century, the play lagged in popularity behind Jonson's better-known *Volpone, The Silent Woman*, and *The Alchemist*. But Quin appeared as Old Kno'well in 1725, and Garrick's version of 1751 – which opened with himself as Kitely and the great clown Harry Woodward as Bobadill – brought it back into the regular repertory. The play was absent from the stage of Drury Lane for only two seasons out of the next 25, and was still being regularly performed there or at Covent Garden until 1802. Edmund Kean played Kitely in 1816, and Mr Macready in 1832 and 1838, but, curiously, the most renowned revival of the nineteenth century was an amateur production of 1845 – with the novelist Charles Dickens hugely acclaimed in the role of Bobadill. Since then the play has not been much in favour, though there has been one earlier production in Stratford – at the Shakespeare Memorial Theatre (as the Royal Shakespeare Theatre was then known), to celebrate the tercentenary of Jonson's death in 1937, directed by Ben Iden Payne, with Donald Wolfit as Bobadill. The last London revival was in 1960, when Joan Littlewood directed the play with her Theatre Workshop company at the 'other' Stratford, in the East End.

Synopsis

Accompanied by his foolish country cousin Stephen, Edward Kno'well sets out for the City from his home in Hoxton, to meet his young friend Wellbred at the Windmill Tavern – but his anxious father, Old Kno'well, has intercepted the letter of invitation, and decides to keep an eye on whatever develops. No less suspicious of Wellbred's man-about-town ways are his brother-in-law Kitely, with whom he lives, and his half brother, the plain Squire Downright. They particularly object to his acquaintance with the plagiaristic poet Matthew and the incurably boastful swordsman Bobadill, who lodges below his would-be stations with the water-carrier Cob and his wife Tib. Brainworm, Kno'well's wily servant, has meanwhile put on the disguise of an old soldier, and, having fooled both his old and young master, decides to take a hand in manipulating events.

Kitely is fearful for the virtue of his young wife and his sister Bridget in a house so often frequented by gulls and gallants. He puts his trust in his servant Cash, who duly dispatches Cob in search of Kitely when the party from the Windmill arrives. Cob tracks down Kitely at the house of the quirky but fair-minded Justice Clement, and takes the opportunity to obtain a warrant against Bobadill, with whom he has quarrelled over the virtues of tobacco. Matthew has meanwhile been making poetical overtures to Bridget, which Young Kno'well and Wellbred mockingly encourage, to the disgust of Downright – and the distraction of the returned Kitely, who assumes Edward to have made him a cuckold.

But Edward has himself fallen in love with Bridget, and while he and Wellbred depart to arrange a secret marriage, Brainworm diverts attention by making Cob's house the focus of Kitely's suspicions. The resulting recriminations lead the party to seek the mediation of Justice Clement, at whose house Bobadill and Matthew are seeking a warrant against Downright, who has soundly beaten both of them. In spite of the compounded deceptions which Brainworm now confesses, Clement commends him for his wit, and chirpily dispenses his own brand of justice. The newly-married Edward and Bridget are reconciled with their various relations, as is Kitely with his wife, and the party adjourns for a celebratory supper.

> 'In no other play is the day so elaborately mapped out; Jonson must have worked out a time-table.'
> *C. H. Herford and Percy and Evelyn Simpson (1950)*

Ben Jonson: a Brief Chronology

1572 Born, 11 June, after the death of his father. His mother remarried a master-bricklayer of Westminster, c.1575, and Jonson was 'brought up poorly' in his early childhood.

1583 c. Educated at Westminster School under the scholar William Camden, until c.1589.

1590 c.Brief and unhappy apprenticeship to his stepfather, after which he went as a volunteer to fight for the Dutch against the Spanish in Flanders, until c.1592.

1595 c. Married Anne Lewis, 'a shrew yet honest'. By this date he was probably acting with a strolling company.

1597 Actor and playwright in London under the manager Philip Henslowe; imprisoned for two months for his share in the 'lewd' and 'seditious' lost comedy *The Isle of Dogs*.

1598 First success with *Every Man in His Humour*, played by the Lord Chamberlain's Men. Killed a fellow actor in a duel, for which he was imprisoned and his goods confiscated. Became a Catholic while in prison. *The Case Is Altered* performed by the Children of the Chapel.

1599 *Every Man out of His Humour*, played by the Chamberlain's Men, antagonized other dramatists by its satire, so beginning the 'war of the the theatres'.

1601 *Cynthia's Revels* and *The Poetaster*, for the Children of the Chapel Royal, continued the 'war', and brought threats of prosecution. Jonson retired temporarily from the stage.

1603 Death of Elizabeth I, and accession of James I. Jonson's first surviving tragedy, *Sejanus*, unsuccessful, and aroused suspicions of 'papist' tendencies. Death from the plague of his only son, Benjamin, aged seven.

1604 Collaborated with Chapman and Marston on *Eastward Ho!* Satirical references to the king's Scots countrymen landed Jonson in prison again.

1605 *The Masque of Blackness*, first of many such courtly pageants of dance and music which Jonson wrote for James I.

1606 *Volpone* performed at the Globe by the King's Men.

1610 *Epicoene* played by the Children of the Queen's Revels, and *The Alchemist* by the King's Men at the Globe. Abjured his Catholicism.

1611 His second and last tragedy, *Catiline*, played by the King's Men.

1612 Travelled to France as tutor to the son of Sir Walter Raleigh.

1614 *Bartholomew Fair* performed at the Hope Theatre.

1616 *The Devil Is an Ass*, Jonson's last play for nine years, during which he devoted his energies to writing further court masques, and some poetry, following the granting of a royal pension. First playwright to publish his collected plays, as *The Works*.

1618 Walked all the way from London to Scotland to visit the Scots poet Drummond of Hawthornden, who recorded their *Conversations* under that title.

1619 Made honorary Master of Arts by Oxford University.

1623 His library destroyed by fire. Contributed a verse tribute to the collected first folio of Shakespeare's works.

1625 Death of James, and accession of the less generous Charles I.

1626 First of Jonson's last group of comedies, *The Staple of News*, for the King's Men.

1628 Confined by paralysis to his chambers, where he was attended by a coterie of disciples, the so-called 'Tribe of Ben'. Appointed City Chronologer of London.

1629 *The New Inn* played by the King's Men.

1630 Quarrelled with Inigo Jones, which further diminished his favour with the court.

1632 *The Magnetic Lady* played by the King's Men.

1633 *A Tale of a Tub* played by Queen Henrietta's Men. None of these later plays proved successful with their audiences.

1637 Died, 6 August, and buried in Westminster Abbey.

'The reputation of Jonson has been of the most deadly kind that can be compelled upon the memory of a great poet. To be universally accepted; to be damned by the praise that quenches all desire to read the book; to be afflicted by the imputation of the virtues which excite the least pleasure; and to be read only by historians and antiquaries – this is the most perfect conspiracy of approval.'

T. S. Eliot (1932)

The Elizabethan Jonson

We tend to think of Ben Jonson as a distinctively Jacobean writer – which in many ways, as a mature playwright, he was. But his earliest years as a dramatist, which include the writing of the first version of *Every Man in His Humour* in 1598 and end with the failure of his tragedy *Sejanus* in 1603 (the year of the old queen's death), give us a picture of an emerging theatre professional of the late-Elizabethan period. Full of developing ideas about both the nature and status of his art, circumstances forced him to acknowledge that it was also a craft – a trade, from which he had a difficult living to earn, and in which he must be ready to turn his hand to any project which offered an honest (or sometimes a slightly scandalous) reward.

The later, Jacobean Jonson disowned or overlooked much of his apprentice work – including whatever plays caused Francis Meres to describe him as among 'our best for Tragedie' as early as 1598. And in the *Conversations* with Jonson recorded by Drummond of Hawthornden some twenty years later, the playwright declared that half his comedies were not in print. Even *The Case Is Altered*, a comedy of romantic intrigue and Jonson's only extant work before *Every Man in His Humour*, would have been lost to us but for an unauthorized edition printed in 1609, and most of his other early work is known to us only by title – though *The Isle of Dogs*, written in 1597 with Thomas Nashe and others, landed him in jail for its 'very seditious and sclandrous matter', so was presumably a satirical comedy.

In 1598, Henry Chettle and Henry Porter were Jonson's collaborators in *Hot Anger Soon Cold* which, on the evidence of its title and of Porter's only surviving single-handed play, was probably a comedy of middle-class marital misunderstandings. *Page of Plymouth*, written in 1599 with Thomas Dekker, was evidently based on a contemporary murder trial, an attempt to make a domestic tragedy out of journalistic opportunism. And in the same year Jonson worked with Dekker, Chettle, and possibly Marston on *Robert II, King of Scots*, which – despite its alternative title of *The Scots Tragedy* – presumably pandered to the late-Elizabethan taste for history plays, since Robert II seems to have lived, for his times, a relatively placid life.

Jonson made a foray into more familiar historical territory in 1602, with *Richard Crookback*, and in the same year there appeared in print a new edition of the old blood-and-guts favourite, Kyd's *Spanish Tragedy*, with five new passages added – for which the manager Philip Henslowe records payments to Jonson. Some modern critics have argued on stylistic grounds that these are unlikely to have been Jonson's work: contrariwise, one may suppose that a skill in stylistic pastiche is precisely what might be expected of a master playwright not yet able to refuse commissions to speak except in his own voice.

Of the early plays which have survived – thanks to Jonson giving them the personal *imprimatur* of inclusion in his collected works – only three comedies besides *Every Man in His Humour* were staged before James's accession: its 'sequel', *Every Man out of His Humour* (1599), and Jonson's two further incursions into that war, *Cynthia's Revels* and *The Poetaster* (both 1600-01). In 1603 came the death of Elizabeth, the failure of the first of Jonson's two surviving tragedies, *Sejanus* – and the death from plague of his only son, Benjamin. In a supremely moving poem, Jonson mourned the loss of this 'child of my right hand, and joy', his father's 'best piece of poetry', and confronted the personal and political realities of the new age.

> 'With *Every Man in His Humour*, Jonson takes a huge step forward. The uncertainty stamped on nearly every page of *The Case Is Altered* has almost vanished; only an occasional clumsiness, an infrequent breach of decorum, betray the hand of the apprentice. Each character now possesses his own idiom, and is revealed by it: Jonson bids his character speak, and they tell us what they are. When he came to revise the play for inclusion in the folio of 1616, he found much to add, but little to change.'
>
> *Jonas A. Barish (1960)*

> 'The theory implicit in *Every Man in His Humour* is clearly that of the New Comedy. The theme does not concern the State at large, nor does it publicly attack those in authority. It does, however, reveal the life of the times, and the customs and manners of the people. In thus attempting to perceive and reveal the truth about human nature, it naturally discloses the vanity and weakness current in society.'
>
> *Henry Holland Carter (1921)*

> 'By the end of Jonson's first act, there are four major intrigues under way: (1) the deception of the elder Knowell by his son; (2) the gulling of Stephen; (3) the trials of Cob; (4) the gulling of Matthew and Bobadill. With Act II, the fifth complication, the Kitely affair, begins. Other characters are successively presented, and always in such a way as to involve them in intrigues already begun, just as characters already active in one intrigue become auxiliaries in another. . . . Clement's laughing tribute to the chief machinator, Brainworm, may seem to point to a Latin model, but no wily slave ever had so many strings to his bow, nor so many gulls to make sport of.'
>
> *Freda L. Townsend (1947)*

Jonson, the Theatres – and the 'War'

Unlike Shakespeare, who was a leading shareholder in the Chamberlain's-King's Men, Ben Jonson was never formally attached to any theatre company. Although the majority of his mature comedies were presented by the King's Men, he remained a freelance all his life, and the theatres where his earlier work was performed, and the companies playing in them, covered a wide spectrum of Elizabethan theatre. The Curtain, where *Every Man in His Humour* probably had its first performance, was in London's first 'theatre district', close by the original Theatre in Shoreditch, outside the northern boundary of the disapproving City of London. When the King's Men moved south of the river to Bankside in 1599, their new Globe Theatre was not only a close neighbour to the Rose and the Swan, but handy for bear-baiting and the brothels besides. All these, of course, were outdoor (or 'public') playhouses, in which the 'groundlings' crowded into the pit-area or yard around a projecting apron stage, only the encircling tiered galleries offering, at a higher price, some protection from the weather.

Jonson's early collaborative work, *The Isle of Dogs*, was performed at the Swan by a group calling themselves Pembroke's Men, of which as little is known as about the play itself: but most of Jonson's apprentice work was as a hack for Philip Henslowe, manager of the chief rivals to the Chamberlain's company – the Lord Admiral's Men, who had been playing since 1594 at the Rose. Henslowe opened the new Fortune Theatre in 1600, probably in response to the closer competition from the Chamberlain's Men at the Globe: and at one or other of Henslowe's theatres were staged all the lost plays in which Jonson had a hand around the turn of the century.

The 'sequel' to our play, *Every Man out of His Humour* would, however, have been among the first plays to have been performed at the new Globe, and it was this play which reputedly sparked the 'war of the theatres'. This was a confusing affair, in which neither the issues nor even the antagonists always can be pinned down: but it does highlight the popularity around this time of the various companies of child players – the 'little eyases' mentioned so slightingly in *Hamlet* (c.1601). There was, indeed, considerable rivalry between the adult companies in the 'public' theatres and the boy companies. From their other duties as choristers, these child actors were able to perform indoors, in the more comfortable and (because also more expensive) socially 'select' conditions of the so-called 'private' houses – where a seat in the benched pit was more expensive than a place in the galleries, from which the 'end-on' staging made for a more restricted view.

It was allegedly a reference in *Every Man out of His Humour* to the 'fustian' of John Marston's plays which caused Marston to hit back by satirizing Jonson in his *Jack Drum's Entertainment*, performed by the Children of Paul's. Jonson responded with *Cynthia's Revels*, which added Dekker to Marston as its targets. This was performed by a second boy company, the Children of the Chapel, who played at Blackfriars (where, incidentally, they leased their premises from the Chamberlain's manager, Richard Burbage, who took his own company there for winter performances after 1609). In 1601, at the height of the 'war', Marston retaliated with *What You Will* and Dekker with *Satiromastix*, both Paul's plays – Jonson intervening with *The Poetaster*, played by the Children of the Chapel.

Although the Chamberlain's Men also performed *Satiromastix*, the war between the dramatists was thus essentially fought out at the private theatres – the grievances of the adult companies having more to do with the threat to their very livelihood from the fashion for child playing, which forced them to find audiences outside London (as far afield as Elsinore!). Indeed, some modern writers have suggested that the whole affair was largely a publicity stunt, designed to promote the interests of all involved – or even a sort of deliberate, dialectic experiment in the new satirical style. By 1604, at least, not only was a truce evidently in force, but Marston was dedicating his play *The Malcontent* to his old 'enemy' Jonson, and, along with Chapman, collaborating with him on *Eastward Ho!* This play landed both Chapman and Jonson in prison for its satirical references to the new King James's nationality (and his notorious sale of honours), and so was partly responsible for the loss of royal patronage by the Children of the Chapel, who performed it. But by this time the fashion for child-playing was on the wane, and Jonson himself, while finding courtly favour with the first of his masques, was turning to the King's Men for the performance of *Sejanus* (1603) and *Volpone* (1606) at the Globe.

'One of the problems with Jonson is that we're in a romantic era, particularly a romantic era of criticism. . . . That is to say, in a play you look for the moment of the turn of the head, the gesture made as the door closes, the way a certain line hangs in the air. . . . It's looking for moments of lyricism. Or insight that is carried by a small, individual, often anarchically placed moment in a play. Shakespeare's full of this. . . . What makes Jonson very exciting for me is that he's a man involved with form. And involved with anarchic life – not of the whole structure of the play, but of the individuals within that play. So consequently his great virtue is not that little turn of the head as you're going through the door, but a great thundering group thing towards a particular idea.'

Terry Hands (1972)

Every Man His Own Editor

For many Elizabethan and Jacobean dramatists, publication of their plays was far from desirable – if not contractually forbidden, as in the one surviving agreement between a playwright and his company, in which Jonson's *protégé* Richard Brome promised the King's Men to put none of his work into print without their permission. For no company wished thus to put into the public domain a play over which it could otherwise claim exclusive ownership. Publication may in some cases thus suggest that a play was nearing the end of its useful life on the stage – though dire economic conditions could also force plays into print, as during the bad plague years of 1636-37, when acting was banned, or during the puritan closure of the theatres, from 1642 to 1660. At that time no fewer than 34 previously unpublished plays attributed to Beaumont and Fletcher were put before a reading public which could no longer see them performed.

The very claim of these latter plays to be the *Collected Works* of their authors, and even the gathering of Shakespeare's plays into the first folio of 1623, was in part thanks to the example of Ben Jonson. In spite of his frequent association with the King's Men, Jonson not only remained a freelance writer all his life, but was far more concerned than any of his fellow dramatists with the need to create a 'literary' status for the drama – and so, incidentally, to ensure the survival of his own reputation for posterity. His publication of all his acknowledged plays in a collected edition in 1616 – dignified as *The Works*, a title usually reserved for the classics, or at least for theological or philosophical writings – was thus unprecedented, and widely regarded as presumptuous.

Such of Shakespeare's plays as were published in single editions during his lifetime, even when they have some appearance of being authorized rather than pirated editions, bear little real evidence of preparation for the press, let alone of special attention being paid to the needs of the reader. Jonson, by contrast, was scrupulously concerned about such details of publication as punctuation (rhetorical as well as grammatical), act and scene division, elaboration of the 'dramatis personae', and the like. Even the first, quarto edition of *Every Man in His Humour*, which appeared in 1601, was dignified with a Latin motto on its title-page: more important, because Jonson changed the setting of his play from Florence to London for the text as published in the folio, the two versions provide a unique opportunity to examine the mind of the writer at work.

Characteristically, Jonson's revision was a far more thorough-going affair than a mere juggling with place names and topical allusions. On the contrary, so concerned was he to retain the integrity of the play as his 'first fruits', that he was careful *not* to make the second version more topical to its date of revision – and dating the revision has, in consequence, provided a happy hunting-ground for scholarly conjecture ever since. Jonson's earliest authoritative editors, Herford and Simpson, firmly declared for a date around 1612, while later scholars have more tentatively suggested almost every year between 1604 and 1614, the prologue alone being attributable with more certainty to 1612.

Our revised text of *Every Man in* thus represents the careful working-over of an early play by a writer concerned to preserve its essential character, but believing no less firmly in the value of substituting a London setting. Whether or not this suggests a date later than 1606, when Jonson was still content to place *Volpone* in Venice, is arguable: but there is surely some significance in the fact that he chose to set not only this revision but every one of his comedies from *The Silent Woman* (1610) onwards in his native city – again by contrast with Shakespeare, whose comedies never venture nearer the metropolis than the rather special circumstances of Windsor, and more usually remain safely if somewhat imprecisely abroad. Jonson's choice had in turn to do with the kind of characters and themes he was writing about – in what *Every Man in* first encapsulates as 'comedies of humours'.

'Jonson's structure is also *independent of the ground;* it is a separate world. It has the perfect structure, the surface tension and iridescence, of a large bubble, but a bubble so constructed that by the laws of its own dynamic it must explode the second, it becomes a whole. Jonson's plays blow themselves out of existence; their resolution is necessarily their end. This is true of his 'prentice bubble-blowing in *Every Man in His Humour*. The characters are *in* their Humour, and then *out*, and there is nothing more to be said.'

Arthur Sale (1949)

'What an extraordinary act of judgement and re-creation is his revision of the Quarto *Every Man in His Humour* for its inclusion in the *Workes*! It would be hard to find a more illuminating example of a great Renaissance poet at the painful business of turning and true-filing his lines and striking a second heat upon the Muse's anvil. He excises the abstract, clarifies the obscure, compresses the sprawling, slashes away the irrelevant, however beautiful it is (such as the eulogy to poetry in the final scene), tightens the syntax and, all the time, with judicious care, works to achieve that "propriety of speech" which Pepys was to find so remarkable fifty years later.'

E. B. Partridge (1972)

'Comedy of Humours' and the Humour of Comedy

Generations of undergraduates have learnt by heart the lines about 'humours' spoken by the Jonson-persona in the induction to *Every Man out of His Humour* (1599) – a 'sequel' to our play only in its variation on the title, not in its characters or plot. In so doing they may impress their examiners, but probably mystify themselves. For, although Jonson concedes the origin of the term in the antiquated medical belief that the human disposition was determined by the balance of 'humours' – the supposed bodily fluids, 'choler, melancholy, phlegm, and blood' – he also stresses that in his plays 'humour' has the generalized sense of 'some one peculiar quality' which so possesses a person as to determine his actions. A 'humour' for Jonson is, in short, a 'singular disposition' – a degree of quirkiness or eccentricity, actual or affected, by embodying which a person reduces himself to a type. From punks to Sloane Rangers, or yuppies to young fogeys, people continue to affect 'humours' today – and continue, in so doing, to make themselves the targets of satirical comedy.

But whereas the conventional modern assumption suggests that it is the uniqueness of an individual's personal traits or temperamental make-up which makes him interesting, in life or art, this is arguably no more than leftover romanticism dignified by the 'science' of psychology. Whether following Aristotle or in blissful ignorance of his neo-classical apologists, pre-romantic artists were concerned rather with the task of portraying what was *typical* – and so universally true – in human nature. Thus, the popular Jacobean prose form of 'character writing' did not offer 'profiles' of individuals in the modern sense, but essayistic descriptions of types: the parson, the actor, the traveller, the hack poet, the dancer, the gull – or, at the level of more serious enquiry, the courtier, or the prince, whose qualities a Castiglione or a Machiavelli had earlier and so influentially tried to define.

It's important to stress this aim of 'typicality' in Jacobean writing, if only because Shakespeare (in Jonson's own tribute) made himself 'not of an age, but for all time' by so often departing from it. Jonson himself is often concerned less with typicality than with the 'typically' eccentric. But there's nothing unusual about this. It has been a method of comedy from Aristophanes to *The Young Ones* (the characters of which were duly berated by their visiting parents for not being in a 'nice' sitcom, such as respectable audiences have always preferred). Chaucer and the Wakefield Master knew about 'humours' technique, too: all Jonson did, with that flair for self-promotion he displayed throughout his life, was to find a catchy new label for an age-old way of making people laugh.

Not, contrary to our expectations, that an educated Jacobean audience would have necessarily agreed that comedy was *about* making people laugh: that, for contemporary critics, was more especially the less dignified concern of farce. Comedy, rather, was about people of a lowlier station in life than tragedy, and, of course, it ended happily – usually, true to the supposed origin of the form in fertility rituals, in a bevy of marriages. Jonson, by that definition, is a more 'modern' writer of comedy than Shakespeare – whose works in the comic form achieve wonders of reconciliation, and may be all about the restoration of social order and so forth, but are not exactly a bundle of laughs. So the only difficulty about the concept of 'humours' is the need to understand that the term is a deliberate misapplication of a misconceived medical notion, and has nothing much to do with the modern meaning of 'humour' – yet at the same time to acknowledge that, by contrast with Shakespearian comedy, Jonson's has everything to do with being funny, in the Jacobean, the modern, or any other sense of the word.

Bergson suggested that the source of laughter was rigidity – the inability of the mind to react with sufficient flexibility to a given situation: and that is arguably the clearest and funniest aspect of many of Jonson's characters. Shakespeare's 'comic' characters, on the other hand, tend to become less funny in inverse proportion to their complexity – or, if you like, to their flexibility. For Shakespeare, this is often tied up with matters of class: such laughter as there is derives from the low-life scenes of the sub-plots, or from a 'magical' rigidity imposed by disguise or the powers of faery. Jonson seldom condescends in this way. True to comic decorum, he does not often deal with the better classes of society: and his ordinary, middle- and working-class characters, whatever their faults, are what they are. In spite of the didactic intentions Jonson proclaimed in prologues, inductions and other critical bits-and-pieces such as Shakespeare assiduously refrained from writing, the people of his plays perkily transcend their supposed flaws and failures, to remain triumphantly or bathetically unchanged by their experiences.

'In our play, Brainworm *is* the plot; he is the key to the right ordering of the pieces of the puzzle, but it is useless to talk of *motive* in connection with him; the plot is one of the Humours in action: the Humour, by finally overreaching itself, is put out of action. Which is exactly the dramatist's purpose for the play as a whole. But it is absurd to talk of Brainworm's motive apart from his Humour. His Humour *is* the one and only motive.'

Arthur Sale (1949)

'Persons such as Comedy Would Choose'

Probably as often quoted as Jonson's definition of 'humours' in *Every Man out* is his declaration of the aims of comedy in the prologue to *Every Man in*. If the spirit of his comedy is Aristophanic, the moral intentions made overt here – to 'show an image of the times' and 'sport with human follies, not with crimes' – derive from Aristotle and Cicero. And the typology of his characters is closer to that of Greek New Comedy than Old, as received through the Roman comedies of Plautus and Terence. Thus, Jonson offers us in *Every Man in* his own variations on the suspicious father (Kno'well), the errant son (Edward), the wily servant (Brainworm), the braggart soldier (Bobadill), the would-be poet (Matthew), and the gull (Stephen). The play seems only to lack a rival, geriatric suitor and a pair of whores (one predatory, the other golden-hearted) to complete the leading roll-call of classical sitcom.

Yet, examined closely, these characters aren't very 'true to type' at all. If old Kno'well has a humour, it is surely no worse than over-protectiveness – while Brainworm manipulates the plot not for his own material gain, but apparently, in a spirit of pure mischief. And if the play sets up expectations reminiscent of a Roman comedy – of an aged father about to be outwitted by a lovesick son and his clever servant – it soon becomes clear that Kno'well's pursuit and even Edward's eventual marriage are no more than incidental to the assembling of a whole gallery of gulls, whose paths cross and recross less in the interests of plot than of the revelation of follies and foibles.

None of the characters, moreover, is subjected to punishment of real severity at the end: indeed, in revising the play from its Italianate to its London setting, Jonson actually replaced a harsh and humiliating punishment for Matthew and Bobadill with their more or less symbolic banishment from the celebratory supper. True, Matthew may be more rigorously discountenanced by the consignment of his poetry to the flames, but Bobadill, that strutting, public-bar version of Falstaff, bounces back after every put-down with a reconstruction of his own view of events that achieves a kind of comic dignity. Kitely may perhaps be diagnosed as suffering from the 'medically' humorous complaint of melancholia – and Jonson's revision of his final scene only increases one's sense that he is far from cured of it, as, after addressing his innocent wife with some perfunctory pentameters of forgiveness, he breaks back into prose with the final, metatheatrical grumble: 'I ha' learned so much verse out of a jealous man's part, in a play.'

Whereas Jonson's earlier, disowned comedy *The Case Is Altered* (*c*.1598) amalgamated two Plautine originals into its somewhat conventional intrigues, *Every Man in* has no known source for its plot; and, in changing its setting to London, Jonson was in effect associating the play with those Jacobean 'city comedies' of Marston, Middleton, and others, in which the metropolis itself becomes almost a 'character' in the day-to-day affairs of middle-class urban life, and 'plot' is little more than a vehicle for the critical display of modern moods and manners. Yet, as Gabriele Bernhard Jackson has persuasively argued, the *characters* seem no more concerned with this specificity of their surroundings than they are (in any truly reciprocal sense) with each other. We recognize in these people, she suggests, 'the inherent capacity of every mind to retreat, as it does in extreme joy or extreme pain, deep into itself, and there to relate every event to its own pleasure or suffering'. Jonson does not go quite as far as Pinter in predicating this solipsism dramaturgically: his characters *seem* to respond to what the previous speaker has just said, and *seem* to share a verifiable universe. But the comedy as often derives from the unstudied irrelevance of a reply as from a pertinent retort: for these characters' minds are prone to be engaged elsewhere, usually deep inside their own heads. And their solipsism actually becomes more rather than less funny if we happen to believe, as did Jonson, in a verifiable universe. Few people in the play, at least, seem to be living there.

'From the moment Knowell strikes the keynote in his opening lines by making Brainworm the bearer of his own paternal authority, each major character conducts his important relationships through a go-between. Brainworm shuttles back and forth between Knowell and Edward; Edward's courtship is conducted by Wellbred; Kitely sends his reprimand to Wellbred through Downright, whom he also uses as a stand-in at the connubial breakfast table; Kitely makes Cash his informant about his wife – and Cash delegates the position to Cob; Bobadill attacks Downright through a law clerk, whom he approaches through Matthew, and serves the resulting warrant by intermediary. . . . The need to interact is a challenge Jonson's characters cannot meet, and it is just this disability which really interests Jonson.'

Gabriel Bernhard Jackson (1969)

'Shakespeare scarcely concerns himself with the legitimacy of his dukes and princes; he simply assumes it. Jonson tends to ponder the credentials of his judges and magistrates, investing them with legal power but not necessarily equivalent moral authority. In *Every Man in His Humour* Judge Clement possesses the official status of a justice of the peace, but also the madcap personality of a Simon Eyre. It is the former that allows him to settle the confusions among the dramatis personae, but the latter that confers on his judgements their humanity and corrective wisdom.'

Jonas A. Barish (1972)

'Deeds and Language such as Men Do Use'

Samuel Pepys recorded in his diary for 9 February 1667 that he had been reading 'a piece of a play, *Every Man in His Humour*, wherein is the greatest propriety of speech that ever I read in my life: and so to bed.' Jonson would have been pleased with the compliment: 'propriety', like 'decorum', had not yet been overlaid with Victorian assumptions of 'respectability', but rather implied fitness, or appropriateness. Nor would Jonson have regarded his choice of prose rather than verse as the dominant medium for *Every Man in* as in any way diminishing his own status as a *poet*. After all, Aristotle himself had been concerned with dramatic and narrative rather than lyric poetry, and had regarded the function of *imitation* as its essential quality. As Jonson himself put it, 'He is called a poet, not he which writeth in measure only, but that fameth or formeth a fable.' In an age before the novel was fully-formed (let alone self-aware), the drama, in prose or in verse, remained the chief story-telling medium.

The point is worth stressing because as Jonson said to Drummond, 'No glass renders a man's form, or likeness, so true as his speech' – yet Jonson himself was equally adept at rendering dramatic speech through prose, as (largely) he did here and in *Bartholomew Fair*, or through the blank verse he employs in *Volpone* or *The Alchemist*. In Shakespeare, the choice of verse or prose is, as so often, a signifier of class – of social (and therefore, for Shakespeare, dramatic) status. But Jonson can convey the language of the highest or lowest with equal facility – even if elevated status in Jonson is as likely to be a matter of pretension as of true rank.

Jonas A. Barish, who has written the fullest account of Jonson's style, tells us that in both versions of *Every Man in His Humour* prose predominates over verse in a ratio of roughly four to one. But whereas the earlier text displays a recurrent concern with the issue of 'good' versus 'bad' poetry, the revision lays much less stress on Edward Kno'well's poetical inclinations, and lets off the poetasting Matthew with a caution. A comparison of the two versions, suggests Barish, shows Jonson honing his vocabulary to denote character with greater precision and complexity. Barish notes in particular the 'sadistic rasp' now discernible in Edward Kno'well's speeches, as his function shifts from that of a commentator upon poetry to a critic of other people. And Anne Barton notes the irony of that sworn enemy of poetry, Old Kno'well, more often employing blank verse than any other character in the play.

Jonson's prologue ridicules other ways in which his fellow playwrights offend against his own sense of correctness. He is especially scornful of history plays such as Shakespeare's, which sweep extensively through time and place, offending against those neo-classical unities left unstressed by Aristotle. Now, we may feel we know better how to value Shakespeare's unruly techniques: yet we probably undervalue, in so doing, the advantages which Jonson gained by confining his action here to the waking hours of a single day, within the environs of a single city. Jonson himself arguably offends against the one truly Aristotelian unity, unity of action – for it would take a good deal of special pleading to explain quite how the affairs of Cob and Tib relate other than mechanically to those of the Kno'wells and Stephen, through the intermediary wheeling and dealing of the Kitely household and its hangers-on, who actually come to occupy pride of place in the plotting. Ironically, it is Jonson's observance of the *other* unities, and the achievement of true 'propriety of speech' in his dialogue, which brings . . . not *order*, but a sort of well-made anarchy to these proceedings, as they muddle purposefully rather than 'build' to their climax.

'Jonsonian comedy constantly plays upon its participants the cosmic joke of encouraging each to think himself central, while its author knows that they are every one tangential. . . . Though he is not yet prepared to admit that Clement himself, in a non-interactive universe, must be tangential in his attempt to impose order . . . , he is already drawing characters of stature whose claim to dignity is the degree of their delusion.'

Gabriel Bernhard Jackson (1969)

'Jonson's clear and insistent demarcation of time fulfils a purpose different from that of either Chapman or Shakespeare. Virtually deprived of plot function, unity of time becomes in his hands a way of evoking, in detail, the life of a great, mercantile Renaissance city as it moves through a typical day: from the early morning distribution of fresh water from the conduits, sordid awakenings in small lodging houses, breakfast and social calls, the routine work of warehouses and offices, desultory talk in taverns and ordinaries, to supper and bed. The city is the true centre of the comedy and, to a large extent, its main character. As hour succeeds hour, a series of petty quarrels, misunderstandings, sexual jealousies, and minor infringements of the law . . . grow in certain areas to the point where they require some rough and ready resolution by a justice of the peace. Then they subside, at least temporarily, in sleep.'

Anne Barton (1984)

'Sport with Human Follies, not with Crimes'

The American critic Harry Levin once suggested that Jonson dealt 'with encounters instead of experiences' and appealed 'to judgement instead of sympathy.' Levin was writing in 1938, well before Brechtian ideas had made much impact on the English-speaking theatre, but the kind of distinctions he was making are essentially Brechtian – logically enough, since what Brecht was in part attempting was the liberation of the theatre from its hungover concern with nineteenth-century psychological realism. My earlier suggestion that Jonson also recognized no less clearly than Pinter the way in which many of us live inside our own heads for most of the time is no less relevant to the kaleidoscopic impression made by this playwright – Jonson can no more be *completely* contained within a Pinteresque pigeon-hole than a Brechtian, let alone (as he demonstrably did leave alone) a Shakespearian. He remains, as John Arden (one of the very few present-day dramatists to acknowledge an allegiance) has nicely put it, 'an embarrassment to the tidy mind'.

Arden went on to suggest that Jonson kept his own more fantastic instincts within bounds by employing 'the control of a tight act-and-scene structure'. Jonson's *formal* discipline, in short, is often employed to display *human* discipline in a state of chronic breakdown. Griff Rhys Jones, the comic actor who directed a revival of *The Alchemist* in 1985, spoke at that time about the 'anti-authoritarian, anarchic vein' he recognized in Jonson: 'He has a liking for craziness, whereas Shakespeare has a horror of it. For Shakespeare, madness is frightening, for Jonson, it's funny . . . In Shakespeare there's nothing to live for if anarchy reigns, whereas for Jonson that's where life really has its foundations.'

That anarchic spirit is perhaps most clearly recognizable in Jonson's great mature comedies, notably *The Alchemist* and *Bartholomew Fair* – where the character who is the self-appointed embodiment of justice and order, Adam Overdo, is discountenanced throughout the play, and muffs his climactic attempt to assert his authority when his wife is sick all over the stage. That Jonson was writing in *Bartholomew Fair* a sort of half-concealed critique of Shakespeare's *Measure for Measure* is now generally recognized – and how much more we relish Overdo's bathetic impotence than the omnipotence of the Duke at the end of *Measure*, as he smugly restores his own version of order.

One might also argue for some sly parallels between *Every Man in His Humour* and the second cycle of Shakespeare's history plays, as overtly criticized in the prologue of later date. We believe the two parts of *Henry IV* to have been written just a year or so earlier than our play, so contemporary audiences would surely have recognized that here was *another* father needlessly concerned about the youthful antics of his son – and so would scarcely have fretted, as some modern critics have done, over the histrionic tendencies of Jonson's

Justice Clement. For if Shakespeare's plays want us to recognize the need for a young prince to shake off the influence of a Lord of Misrule, and adopt the tidy values of a Lord Chief Justice, what more elliptic Jonsonian contrast could there be than a humbler magistrate as prone to break into playacting as Falstaff and Prince Hal, dispensing a brand of justice which has precious little to do with the statute book?

It's less remarkable that *Every Man in* should also offer its own version of that age-old stereotype, the braggart soldier: but if Bobadill is undeniably a far less complex a version of this figure than Falstaff, he is also refreshingly less schematic in function. Bobadill has to be disowned by nobody in the overriding interests of an ordered climax – and would probably rise solipsistically above the rebuff if he was. If Falstaff is no 'mere' comic creation, nor yet is Bobadill 'merely' comic – but he is *purely* so. For Jonson does submit his anarchic instinct to his neo-classical intellect to the extent of never trying to 'break the form' of comedy itself – which Aristotle had claimed to be 'an imitation of men worse than the average, not indeed as regards any and every sort of vice, but only the ridiculous, which . . . may be defined as a mistake or deformity which produces no pain or harm to others'. In part Jonson paraphrases this aim in his prologue: *in toto*, he renders it in his play.

There's nothing here, one notices, about characters being *changed* by their experiences, as they usually are by the events of a Shakespearian comedy (often following a symbolic journey from the city to the country – a route which, if anything, is reversed here). Yet again, Jonson is clearly the more realistic writer – and if not the more 'satisfying', then clearly the more Brechtian – in showing that, by and large, people do *not* 'learn from their experiences' in real life in quite the way it has become the dramatic convention to expect that they should. The audience, with whom the final burden of judgement usually rests in a play by Jonson as by Brecht, *may* hopefully learn from what it has seen: if not, it has at least had a good laugh.

To the modern mind, Jonson seems, paradoxically, both intensely conservative and a thoroughgoing radical – conservative in his resolute disbelief in the likelihood of change for the better, but radical in his clearsighted appraisal of the social basis of human behaviour; reactionary in his belief that men do not learn from their experiences, but revolutionary in his recognition that most of the ways in which social constraints are imposed on human wilfulness are themselves corrupt. These conflicting impulses produce a sustained, creative tension in the plays – and an overriding sense of the affirmation of 'untidy' life in all its eccentricities.

For Further Reading

The eleven-volume Oxford edition of *Ben Jonson*, edited by C. H. Herford and P. and E. Simpson (Clarendon Press, 1925-52), remains the most authoritative and complete, though in some respects it is now out-of-date, and not always easy to use. The Everyman edition in two volumes, edited by F. E. Schelling (London: Dent, 1910), has the virtue of completeness and cheapness, but is textually not very sound. The 'Yale Ben Jonson' is the fullest more recent edition, while *Three Comedies* in the Penguin English Library conveniently assembles Jonson's mature masterpieces, *Volpone, The Alchemist* and *Bartholomew Fair*.

Among individual editions of *Every Man in His Humour*, that edited by J. W. Lever in the Regents Renaissance Drama Series (London: Arnold, 1972) helpfully provides parallel texts of the quarto and folio versions. M. Seymour-Smith has edited the play for the New Mermaid series (London: Benn, 1966), while the Yale edition (New Haven, Conn.: Yale University Press, 1969) contains a stimulating introduction by G.B. Jackson.

Marchette Chute's *Ben Jonson of Westminster* (New York: Dutton, 1953) is a readable, generally reliable biography. On the sociohistorical background, L.C. Knights's *Drama and Society in the Age of Jonson* (London: Chatto and Windus, 1937) remains essential, if only to spark disagreement, while Andrew Gurr's *The Shakespearean Stage* (Cambridge University Press, second edition, 1980) assembles most of the available information on the theatre and staging conditions, combining concision and readability. Other useful background works include M. C. Bradbrook's *The Growth and Structure of Elizabethan Comedy* (London: Cassell, 1955); Brian Gibbons's *Jacobean City Comedy* (London: Methuen, second edition, 1980); and two complementary volumes in the 'Theatre Production Studies' series, Michael Hattaway's *Elizabethan Popular Theatre* and Peter Thomson's *Shakespeare's Theatre* (London: Routledge, 1982 and 1983).

Three collections of essays usefully assemble the best shorter pieces on Jonson's work. *Ben Jonson: a Collection of Critical Essays* (Englewood Cliffs, N.J.: Prentice-Hall, 1963) includes the highly influential evaluation by T.S. Eliot; the odd, pseudo-Freudian put-down by Edmond Wilson; Harry Levin's essay cited in this introduction; and Arthur Sale's introduction to his own edition of *Every Man in His Humour. The Elizabethan Theatre IV*, edited by G.R. Hibbard (London: Macmillan, 1974), assembles eight papers, including a nice overview by S. Schoenbaum, given at a conference commemorating Jonson's quatercentenary. And *Every Man in His Humour and The Alchemist: a Casebook*, edited by R. V. Holdsworth (London: Macmillan, 1978), collects much elusive historical material on our play, in addition to six modern essays and extracts. A special Jonson issue of the journal *Gambit* (Vol. VI, No.22, 1972) includes one of the few discussions by theatre professionals (Terry Hands, Colin Blakely, and Peter Barnes among them), and also the essay by John Arden from which I have quoted.

Among full-length general studies are J. B. Bamborough's introductory *Ben Jonson* (London: Hutchinson, 1970); Jonas A. Barish's essential *Ben Jonson and the Language of Prose Comedy* (Cambridge, Mass.: Harvard University Press, 1960); Anne Barton's thorough play-by-play study *Ben Jonson, Dramatist* (Cambridge University Press, 1984); J. A. Bryant's *The Compassionate Satirist: Ben Jonson and His Imperfect World* (Athens: University of Georgia Press, 1972); Alan C. Dessen's *Jonson's Moral Comedy* (Evanston, Ill.: Northwestern University Press, 1971); R. Dutton's *Ben Jonson: To The First Folio* (Cambridge University Press, 1983); G. B. Jackson's *Vision and Judgement in Ben Jonson's Drama* (New Haven, Conn.: Yale University Press, 1968); Robert Gale Noye's *Ben Jonson on the English Stage, 1660-1776* (London: Oxford University Press, 1935); A. S. Leggatt's *Ben Jonson: His Vision and his Art* (London: Macmillan, 1981); and E. B. Partridge's valuable *The Broken Compass* (New York: Colombia University Press, 1958).

'Jonson is commonly conceived as a man who wrote comedies because he had a theory about why comedies ought to be written. This formidable misconception is buttressed by Jonson's own words in a tireless series of prefaces, prologues, and asides. To accept them is to take an author's rationalizations about his own work too seriously and to ignore the historical circumstances that they were designed to meet. The comedy of humours was not arrived at as a descriptive formulation for purely critical purposes; it was seized upon as a polemical weapon to answer the Puritan attacks on the stage.'

Harry Levin (1938)

'To an intelligent and sensitive man of any school of thought Shakespeare appears sensitive and intelligent. But Ben Jonson, after Shakespeare, appears neither. Though he attempts a variety of characters, they all boil down to a few motivations, recognizable as the motivations of Jonson himself and rarely transformed into artistic creations. Shakespeare expands himself, breeds his cells as organic beings. . . . Jonson merely splits himself up and sets the pieces – he is to this extent a dramatist – in conflict with one another. . . . Ben Jonson seems an obvious example of a psychological type which has been described by Freud and designated by a technical name, *anal erotic* . . . '

Edmund Wilson (1938)

Also in the RSC's Mermaid Theatre Season   **The Two Noble Kinsmen**

Hugh Quarshie: ARCITE   Gerard Murphy: PALAMON

The Rover

Jeremy Irons: WILLMORE
Sinead Cusack: ANGELLICA BIANCA

Imogen Stubbs: HELLENA

Top left: Imelda Staunton: BESS
Right Joe Melia: MULLISHEG

Imelda Staunton: BESS

Every Man in His Humour, Mermaid Theatre production 1987

Nathaniel Parker: WELLBRED.
Simon Russell Beale: ED KNO'WELL

Pete Postlethwaite: CAPTAIN BOBADILL,
Paul Greenwood: MASTER STEPHEN,
Roger Moss: CLEMENT'S SERVANT,
Simon Russell Beale: ED KNO'WELL

EVERY MAN IN HIS HUMOUR

by Ben Jonson

TO THE MOST LEARNED, AND MY HONOURED FRIEND
Master Camden, CLARENCEUX.

SIR, There are, no doubt, a supercilious race in the world, who will esteem all office, done you in this kind, an injury; so solemn a vice it is with them to use the authority of their ignorance, to the crying down of Poetry, or the Professors: but, my gratitude must not leave to correct their error; since I am none of those, that can suffer the benefits conferred upon my youth, to perish with my age. It is a frail memory, that remembers but present things: and, had the favour of the times so conspired with my disposition, as it could have brought forth other, or better, you had had the same proportion, and number of the fruits, the first. Now, I pray you, to accept this, such, wherein neither the confession of my manners shall make you blush; nor of my studies, repent you to have been the instructor: and, for the profession of my thankfulness, I am sure, it will, with good men, find either praise or excuse.

Your true lover,
BEN JONSON.

The Persons of the Play

KNO'WELL, an old gentleman.
ED. KNO'WELL, his son
BRAINWORM, the father's man
Master STEPHEN, a country gull
{ GEORGE} DOWNRIGHT, a plain squire
WELLBRED, his half-brother
Justice CLEMENT, an old merry magistrate
ROGER FORMAL, his clerk
{ THOMAS} KITELY, a merchant
Dame KITELY, his wife
Mistress BRIDGET, his sister
Master MATTHEW, the town gull
{ THOMAS} CASH, Kitely's man
{ OLIVER} COB, a water-bearer
TIB, his wife
Captain BOBADILL, a Paul's man
{ SERVANTS, etc}

The Scene.
LONDON.

The Text

The text used and reproduced here in full is taken from the edition prepared by M. Seymour-Smith for the New Mermaids series (London: Benn, 1979). In that edition Jonson's own stage directions were retained but were amplified, although minimally. All editorial additions are given between braces. The cuts made in the RSC version are indicated by square brackets in the text. Alterations and additions are indicated at the foot of the page, under the main text.

Prologue

Though need make many Poets, and some such
As art, and nature have not bettered much;
Yet ours, for want, hath not so loved the stage,
As he dare serve th'ill customs of the age:
Or purchase your delight at such a rate,
As, for it, he himself must justly hate.
To make a child, now swaddled, to proceed
Man, and then shoot up, in one beard, and weed,
Past threescore years: or, with three rusty swords,
And help of some few foot-and-half-foot words,
Fight over York, and Lancaster's long jars;
And in the tiring-house bring wounds, to scars.
He rather prays, you will be pleased to see
One such, to-day, as other plays should be.
Whether neither Chorus wafts you o'er the seas;
Nor creaking throne comes down, the boys to please;
Nor nimble squib is seen, to make afeared
The gentlewoman; nor rolled bullet heard
To say, it thunders; nor tempestuous drum
Rumbles, to tell you when the storm doth come;
But deeds, and language, such as men do use:
And persons, such as Comedy would choose,
When she would show an Image of the times,
And sport with human follies, not with crimes.
Except, we make 'hem such by loving still
Our popular errors, when we know they're ill.
[1][I] mean such errors, as you'll all confess
By laughing at them, they deserve no less:
Which when you heartily do, there's hope left, then,
You, that have so graced monsters, may like men.

ACT 1

Scene i

{*A Plot before Kno'well's House.*[2] {*Enter*} *Kno'well.*

KNO'WELL.
    A goodly day toward! And a fresh morning!
                                        Brainworm!

    {*Enter*} *Brainworm.*

    Call up your young master: bid him rise, sir.
    Tell him, I have some business to employ him.

BRAINWORM.
    I will sir, presently.

KNO'WELL.   But hear you, sirrah,
    If he be' at his book, disturb him not.

BRAINWORM.   Well sir.

                          {*Exit Brainworm.*}

KNO'WELL.
    How happy, yet, should I esteem myself
    Could I, by any practice, wean the boy
    From one vain course of study, he affects.
    He is a scholar, if a man may trust
    The liberal voice of fame, in her report
    Of good account, in both our universities,
    Either of which hath favoured him with graces:
    But their indulgence, must not spring in me
    A fond opinion, that he cannot err.
    Myself was once a student; and, indeed,
    Fed with the self-same humour, he is now,
    Dreaming on nought but idle poetry,
    That fruitless, and unprofitable art,
    [Good unto none, but least to the professors,]
    Which, then, I thought the mistress of all knowledge:
    But since, time, and the truth have waked my judgement,
    And reason taught me better to distinguish,
    The vain, from th' useful learnings.

    {*Enter*} *Master Stephen.*

                          Cousin Stephen!

---

[1] We
[2] *Insert: at Hogsden*

What news with you, that you are here so early?

STEPHEN.
Nothing, but e'en come to see how you do, uncle.

KNO'WELL.
That's kindly done, you are welcome, coz.

STEPHEN.
Ay, I know that sir, I would not ha' come else. How do my cousin Edward, uncle?

KNO'WELL.
Oh, well coz, go in and see: I doubt he be scarce stirring yet.

STEPHEN.
Uncle, afore I go in, can you tell me, an' he have e'er a book of the sciences of hawking, and hunting? I would fain borrow it.

KNO'WELL.
Why, I hope you will not a hawking now, will you?

STEPHEN.
No wusse; but I'll practise against next year uncle: I have bought me a hawk, and a hood, and bells, and all; I lack nothing but a book to keep it by.

KNO'WELL.
Oh, most ridiculous.

STEPHEN.
Nay, look you now, you are angry, uncle: why you know, an' a man have not skill in the hawking, and hunting-languages nowadays, I'll not give a rush for him. They are more studied than the Greek, or the Latin. He is for no gallants' company without 'hem. And by [3][gad's lid] I scorn it, I, so I do, to be a consort for every humdrum, hang 'hem scroyles, there's nothing in 'hem, i' the world. What do you talk on it? Because I dwell at Hogsden, I shall keep company with none but the archers of Finsbury? Or the citizens, that come a ducking to Islington ponds? A fine jest i' faith! 'Slid a gentleman mun show himself like a gentleman. Uncle, I pray you be not angry, I know what I have to do, I trow, I am no novice.

KNO'WELL.
You are a prodigal absurd coxcomb: go to.
Nay never look at me, it's I that speak.
Take't as you will sir, I'll not flatter you.
Ha' you not yet found means enow, to waste
That, which your friends have left you, but you must
Go cast away your money on a [4][kite],
And know not how to keep it, when you ha' done?
Oh it's comely! This will make you a gentleman!

Well cousin, well! I see you are e'en past hope
Of all reclaim. Ay, so, now you are told on it,
You look another way.

STEPHEN.
                              What would you ha' me do?

KNO'WELL.
What would I have you do? I'll tell you kinsman,
Learn to be wise, and practise how to thrive,
That would I have you do: and not to spend
Your coin on every bauble, that you fancy,
Or every foolish brain, that humours you.
I would not have you to [5][invade each place,
Nor thrust yourself on all societies,
Till men's affections, or your own desert,
Should worthily invite you to your rank.
He, that is so respectless in his courses,
Oft sells his reputation, at cheap market.]
Nor would I, you should melt away yourself
In flashing bravery, lest while you affect
To make a blaze of gentry to the world,
A little puff of scorn extinguish it,
And you be left, like an unsavoury snuff,
Whose property is only to offend.
I'd ha' you sober, and contain yourself;
Not, that your sail be bigger than your boat:
[But moderate your expenses now, at first,
As you may keep the same proportion still.]
Nor, stand so much on your gentility,
Which is an airy, and mere borrowed thing,
From dead men's dust, and bones: [and none of yours
Except you make, or hold it.][6] Who comes here?

{Enter a} Servant.

SERVANT.
Save you, gentlemen.

STEPHEN.
Nay, we do' not stand much on our gentility, friend; yet, you are welcome and I assure you, mine uncle here is a man of a

---

[3] God's will
[4] Buzzard
[5]   intrude yourself
    In every gentleman's society
    Till their affections, or your own desert,
    Do worthily invite you to your rank.
[6] *Insert:* But

thousand a year, Middlesex land: he has but one son in all the world, I am his next heir, at the common law, Master Stephen, as simple as I stand here, if my cousin die – as there's hope he will – I have a pretty living o' my own too, beside, hard by here.

SERVANT.

In good time, sir.

STEPHEN.

In good time, sir? Why! And in very good time, sir. You do not flout, friend, do you?

SERVANT.

Not I, sir.

STEPHEN.

Not you, sir? You were not best, sir; an' you should, here be them can perceive it, and that quickly too: go to. And they can give it again soundly too, and need be.

SERVANT.

Why, sir, let this satisfy you: good faith, I had no such intent.

STEPHEN.

[7][Sir, an' I thought you had,] I would talk with you, and that presently.

SERVANT.

Good Master Stephen, so you may, sir, at your pleasure.

STEPHEN.

And so I would sir, good my saucy companion! An you were not o' mine uncle's ground, I can tell you; though I do not stand upon my gentility neither in't.

KNO'WELL.

Cousin! cousin! Will this ne'er be left?

STEPHEN.

Whoreson base fellow! A mechanical serving-man! By [8][this cudgel,] and't were not for shame, I would –

KNO'WELL.

What would you do, you peremptory [9][gull?
If you cannot be quiet, get you hence.]
You see, the honest man demeans himself
Modestly to'ards you, [giving no reply
To your unseasoned, quarrelling, rude fashion:]
And, still you huff it, with a kind of carriage,
As void of wit, as of humanity.
Go, get you in; fore [10][heaven] I am ashamed
Thou hast a kinsman's interest in me.

{Exit Stephen.}

SERVANT.

I pray you, sir. Is this Master Kno'well's house?

KNO'WELL.

Yes, marry, it is sir.

SERVANT.

I should enquire for a gentleman, here, one Master Edward Kno'well: do you know any such, sir, I pray you?

KNO'WELL.

I should forget myself else, sir.

SERVANT.

Are you the gentleman? Cry you mercy sir: I was required by a gentleman i' the city, as I rode out at this end o' the town, to deliver you this letter, sir.

KNO'WELL.

To me, sir! What do you mean? Pray you remember your court'sy. {Reads} 'To his most selected friend, Master Edward Kno'well.' What might the gentleman's name be, sir, that sent it? Nay, pray you be covered.

SERVANT.

One Master Wellbred, sir.

KNO'WELL.

Master Wellbred! A young gentleman? Is he not?

SERVANT.

The same sir, Master Kitely married his sister: the rich merchant i' the Old Jewry.

KNO'WELL.

You say very true. Brainworm!

{Enter} Brainworm.

BRAINWORM.

Sir.

KNO'WELL.

Make this honest friend drink here: pray you go in.

{Exeunt Brainworm and Servant.}

This letter is directed to my son:
Yet, I am Edward Kno'well too, and may
With the safe conscience of good manners, use

---

[7] By God, an' I thought you had, sir
[8] God's lid
[9] ass?
[10] God

The fellow's error to my satisfaction.
Well, I will break it ope – old men are curious –
Be it but for the style's sake, and the phrase,
To see, if both do answer my son's praises,
Who is, almost, grown the idolator
Of this young Wellbred: what have we here? [What's this?]
({*Reads*} *the letter*.) 'Why, Ned, I beseech thee; has thou
forsworn all thy friends i' the Old Jewry? [Or dost thou think us
all Jews that inhabit there, yet? If thou dost, come over, and but
see our frippery: change an old shirt, for a whole smock, with
us.] Do not conceive that antipathy between us, and Hogsden;
as was between Jews and hogs-flesh. Leave thy vigilant father,
alone, to number over his green apricots, evening and morning,
o' the north-west wall: an' I had been his son, I had saved him
the labour, long since; if, taking in all the young wenches, that
pass by, at the back-door, and coddling every kernel of the fruit
for 'hem, would ha' served. But, pr'ythee, come over to me,
quickly, this morning: I have such a present for thee [our
Turkey company never sent the like to the Grand Signior]. One
is a rhymer sir, o' your own batch, [your own leaven;] but doth
think himself Poet-major, o' the town: [willing to be shown,
and worthy to be seen.] The other – I will not venture his
description [with you,] till you come, because I would ha' you
make hither with an appetite. [If the worst of 'hem be not worth
your journey, draw your bill of charges, as unconscionable, as
any Guildhall verdict will give it you, and you shall be allowed
your viaticum.]
        From the Windmill.'
From the Bordello, it might come as well;
The Spittle: or Pict-hatch. Is this the man,
My son hath sung so, for the happiest wit,
The choicest brain, the times hath sent us forth?
I know not what he may be, in the arts;
Nor what in schools: but surely, for his manners,
I judge him a profane, and dissolute wretch:
[Worse, by possession of such great good gifts,
Being the master of so loose a spirit.]
Why, what unhallowed ruffian would have writ,
In such a scurrilous manner, to a friend!
Why should he think, I tell my Apricots?
Or play th' Hesperian Dragon, with my fruit,
To watch it? Well, my son, I' had thought
You'd had more judgement, t'have made election
Of your companions, then t'have ta'en on trust,
Such petulant, jeering gamesters, that can spare
No argument, or subject from their jest.
But I perceive, affection makes a fool
Of any man, too much the father. Brainworm!

{*Enter*} *Brainworm.*

BRAINWORM.
    Sir.

KNO'WELL.
    Is the fellow gone that brought this letter?

BRAINWORM.
    Yes, sir, a pretty while since.

KNO'WELL.
    And, where's your young master?

BRAINWORM.
    In his chamber sir.

KNO'WELL.
    He spake not with the fellow! Did he?

BRAINWORM.
    No sir, he saw him not.

KNO'WELL.
    Take you this letter, and deliver it my son, but with no notice,
    that I have opened it, on your life.

BRAINWORM.
    Oh lord, sir, that were a jest, indeed!

                                        {*Exit Brainworm.*}

KNO'WELL.
    I am resolved, I will not stop his journey;
    Nor practise any violent mean, to stay
    The unbridled course of youth in him: for that,
    Restrained, grows more impatient; and, in kind,
    Like to the eager, but the generous greyhound,
    Who ne'er so little from his game withheld,
    Turns head, and leaps up at his holder's throat.
    There is a way of winning, more by love,
    And urging of the modesty, than fear:
    Force works on servile natures, not the free.
    He, that's compelled to goodness, may be good;
    But 'tis but for that fit: where others drawn
    By softness, and example, get a habit.
    Then, if they stray, but warn 'hem: and, the same
    They should for virtue' have done, they'll do for shame.

                                        {*Exit.*}

Scene ii

{*Kno'well's House. Enter*} *Ed. Kno'well, Brainworm.*

ED. KNO'WELL.
> Did he open it, sayest thou?

BRAINWORM.
> Yes, o' my word sir, and read the contents.

ED. KNO'WELL.
> That scarce contents me. What countenance, pr'ythee, made he, i' the reading of it? Was he angry, or pleased?

BRAINWORM.
> Nay sir, I saw him not read it, nor open it, I assure your worship.

ED. KNO'WELL.
> No? How know'st thou, then, that he did either?

BRAINWORM.
> Marry sir, because he charged me, on my life, to tell nobody, that he opened it: which, unless he had done, he would never fear to have it revealed.

ED. KNO'WELL.
> That's true: well I thank thee, Brainworm.

> {*He reads the letter.*}
> {*Enter*} *Master Stephen.*

STEPHEN.
> Oh, Brainworm, did'st thou not see a fellow here in a what-sha'-call-him doublet? He brought mine uncle a letter e'en now.

BRAINWORM.
> Yes, Master Stephen, what of him?

STEPHEN.
> Oh, I ha' such a mind to beat him – Where is he? Canst thou tell?

BRAINWORM.
> Faith, he is not of that mind: he is gone, Master Stephen.

STEPHEN.
> Gone? Which way? When went he? How long since?

BRAINWORM.
> He is rid hence. He took horse, at the street door.

STEPHEN.
> And, I stayed i' the fields! Whoreson scanderbag rogue! Oh that I had a horse [11][to fetch him back again.]

BRAINWORM.
> Why, you may ha' my master's gelding, to save your longing, sir.

STEPHEN.
> But I ha' no boots, that's the spite on't.

BRAINWORM.
> Why, a fine wisp of hay, rolled hard, Master Stephen.

STEPHEN.
> No faith, it's no boot to follow him, now: let him e'en go, and hang. 'Pray thee, help to truss me, a little. He does so vex me –

BRAINWORM.
> You'll be worse vexed, when you are trussed, Master Stephen. Best, keep unbraced; and walk yourself, till you be cold: your choler may founder you else.

STEPHEN.
> By my faith, and so I will, now thou tell'st me on't: how dost thou like my leg, Brainworm?

BRAINWORM.
> A very good leg, Master Stephen! But the woollen stocking does not commend it so well.

STEPHEN.
> Foh, the stockings be good enough, now summer is coming on, for the dust: I'll have a pair of silk again winter, that I go to dwell i' the town. I think my leg would show in a silk-hose.

BRAINWORM.
> Believe me, Master Stephen, rarely well.

STEPHEN.
> In sadness, I think it would: I have a reasonable good leg.

BRAINWORM.
> You have an excellent good leg, Master Stephen, but I cannot stay, to praise it longer now, and I am very sorry for't.

> {*Exit Brainworm.*}

STEPHEN.
> Another time will serve, Brainworm. Gramercy for this.

ED. KNO'WELL.
> Ha, ha, ha! ({*Ed.*} *Kno'well laughs having read the letter.*)

STEPHEN.
> 'Slid, I hope, he laughs not at me, and he do –

---

[11] I'd fetch him back again, with heave and ho

ED. KNO'WELL.

Here was a letter, indeed, to be intercepted by a man's father, [and do him good with him]! He cannot but think most virtuously, both of me, and the sender, sure; [12][that make the careful costermonger of him in our 'familiar Epistles'. Well, if he read this with patience, I'll be gelt, and troll ballads for Master John Trundle, yonder, the rest of my mortality. It is true, and likely,] my father may have as much patience as another man; for he takes [very] much physic: and, oft taking physic makes a man very patient. But would your packet, Master Wellbred, had arrived [at him,] in such a minute of his patience; then, we had known the end of it, which now is doubtful, and threatens – *{Sees Stephen}* What! My wise cousin! *{Aside}* Nay, then, I'll furnish our feast with one gull more to'ard the mess. He writes to me of a brace, and here's one, that's three: Oh, for a fourth; Fortune, if ever thou'lt use thine eyes, I entreat thee –

STEPHEN.

{Aside} Oh, now I see, who he laughed at. He laughed at somebody in that letter. By this good light, and he had laughed at me –

ED. KNO'WELL.

How now, cousin Stephen, melancholy?

STEPHEN.

Yes, a little. I thought, you had laughed at me, cousin.

ED. KNO'WELL.

Why, what an' I had coz, what would you ha' done?

STEPHEN.

By this light, I would ha' told mine uncle.

ED. KNO'WELL.

Nay, if you would ha' told your uncle, I did laugh at you, coz.

STEPHEN.

Did you, indeed?

ED. KNO'WELL.

Yes, indeed.

STEPHEN.

Why, then –

ED. KNO'WELL.

What then?

STEPHEN.

I am satisfied, it is sufficient.

ED. KNO'WELL.

Why, be so gentle coz. And, I pray you let me entreat a courtesy of you. I am sent for, this morning, by a friend i' the Old Jewry to come to him; it's but crossing over the fields to Moorgate: will you bear me company? I protest, it is not to draw you into [bond, or] any plot against the state, coz.

STEPHEN.

Sir, that's all one, and 'twere: you shall command me, twice so far as Moorgate to do you good, in such a matter. Do you think I would leave you? I protest –

ED. KNO'WELL.

No, no, you shall not protest, coz.

STEPHEN.

By my fackins, but I will, by your leave; I'll protest more to my friend, than I'll speak of, at this time.

ED. KNO'WELL.

You speak very well, coz.

STEPHEN.

Nay, not so neither, [you shall pardon me:] but I speak, to serve my turn.

ED. KNO'WELL.

Your turn, coz? Do you know, what you say? A gentleman of your sort, parts, carriage, and estimation, to talk o' your turn i' this company, and to me, alone, like a tankard-bearer, at a conduit! Fie. A wight, that, hitherto, his every foot hath left the stamp of a great foot behind him, [as every word the savour of a strong spirit!] And he! This man! So graced, gilded, or – to use a more fit metaphor – so tin-foiled by nature, [13][as not ten housewives' pewter, again a good time, shows more bright to the world than he!] And he – as I said last, so I say again, and still shall say it – this man! To conceal such real ornaments as these, and shadow their glory, as a milliner's wife does her wrought stomacher, with [a smoky lawn,] or a black cyprus? Oh coz! It cannot be answered, go not about it. Drake's old ship, at Deptford, may sooner circle the world again. Come, wrong not the quality of your desert, with looking downward, coz; but hold up your head, so: and let the Idea of what you are,

---

[12] *Insert:* why, it is able to break the shins of any old man's patience in the world. My father read this with patience? Then I will be made an eunuch, and learn to sing ballads the rest of my mortality. True

[13] *Insert:* not that you have a leaden constitution, coz, although perhaps a little inclining to that temper, and so the more apt to melt with pity, when you fall into the fire of rage; but for your lustre only, which reflects as bright to the world as an old ale-wife's pewter against a good time.

be portrayed i' your face, that men may read i' your physnomy, 'Here, within this place, is to be seen the true, rare, and accomplished monster, or miracle of nature', which is all one. What think you of this, coz?

STEPHEN.

Why, I do think of it; and I will be more proud, and melancholy, and gentleman-like, than I have been: I'll insure you.

ED. KNO'WELL.

Why, that's resolute Master Stephen!
{Aside} Now, if I can but hold him up to his height, as it is happily begun, it will do well for a suburb-humour: we may hap have a match with the [14][city] and play him for forty pound. – Come, coz.

STEPHEN.

I'll follow you.

ED. KNO'WELL.

Follow me? You must go before.

STEPHEN.

Nay, an' I must, I will. Pray you, show me, good cousin.

{Exeunt}

Scene iii

{The Lane before Cob's House. Enter} Matthew.

MATTHEW.

I think, this be the house: what, ho?

Cob {opens door.}

COB.

Who's there? Oh, Master Matthew! Gi' your worship good morrow.

MATTHEW.

What! Cob! How dost thou, good Cob? Dost thou inhabit here, Cob?

COB.

Ay, sir, I and my lineage ha' kept a poor house, here, in our days.

MATTHEW.

Thy lineage, Monsieur Cob, what lineage? What lineage?

COB.

Why sir, an ancient lineage, and a princely. Mine ance'try came

from a King's belly, no worse man: and yet no man neither – by your worship's leave, I did lie in that – but Herring the King of fish, from his belly, I proceed, one o' the Monarchs o' the world, I assure you. The first red herring, that was broiled in Adam, and Eve's kitchen, do I fetch my pedigree from, [by the Harrots' books.] His cob, was my great-great-mighty-great grandfather.

MATTHEW.

Why mighty? Why mighty? I pray thee.

COB.

Oh, it was a mighty while ago, sir, and a mighty great cob.

MATTHEW.

How know'st thou that?

COB.

How know I? Why, I smell his ghost, ever and anon.

MATTHEW.

Smell a ghost? Oh unsavoury jest! And the ghost of a [15][herring-cob!]

COB.

Ay, sir, with favour of your worship's nose, Master Matthew, why not the ghost of a herring-cob, as well as the ghost of rasher-bacon?

MATTHEW.

Roger Bacon, thou would'st say?

COB.

I say rasher-bacon. They were both broiled o' the coals? And a man may smell broiled meat, I hope? You are a scholar, upsolve me that, now.

MATTHEW.

Oh raw ignorance! – Cob, canst thou show me of a gentleman, one Captain Bobadill, where his lodging is?

COB.

Oh, my guest, sir! You mean.

MATTHEW.

Thy guest! Alas! Ha, ha.

COB.

Why do you laugh, sir? Do you not mean Captain Bobadill?

---

[14] city-gull
[15] herring Cob?

MATTHEW.

Cob, 'pray thee, advise thyself well: do not wrong the gentleman, and thyself too. I dare be sworn, he scorns thy house: he! He lodge in such a base, obscure place, as thy house! Tut, I know his disposition so well, he would not lie in thy bed, if thou'dst gi'it him.

COB.

[I will not give it him, though, sir.] Mass, I thought somewhat was in't, we could not get him to bed, all night! Well, sir, though he lie not o' my bed, he lies o' my bench: an't please you to go up, sir, you shall find him with two cushions under his head, and his cloak wrapped about him, [as though he had neither won nor lost, and yet,] I warrant, he ne'er [16][cast] better in his life, than he has done, tonight.

MATTHEW.

Why? Was he drunk?

COB.

Drunk, sir? You hear not me say so. Perhaps, he swallowed a tavern[-token], or some such device, sir: I have nothing to do withal. I deal with water, and not with wine. [Gi'me my tankard there, ho.

{Enter Tib with tankard, and exit.}]

God b'w'you, sir. It's six o'clock; I should ha' carried two turns, by this. What ho! My [17][stopple!] Come.

MATTHEW.

Lie in a water-bearer's house! A gentleman of his havings! Well, I'll tell him my mind.

COB.

What Tib, show this gentleman up to the Captain.

{Enter Tib with [18][stopple] and exit with Matthew.}

[Oh, an' my house were the Brazen-head now! Faith, it would e'en speak, 'Moe fools yet'.] You should ha' some now would take this Master Matthew to be a gentleman, at the least. His father's an honest man, a worshipful fishmonger, and so forth; and now does he creep, and wriggle into acquaintance with all the brave gallants about the town, such as my guest is [– Oh, my guest is a fine man –] and they flout him invincibly. He useth every day to a merchant's house, where I serve water, one Master Kitely's, i' the Old Jewry; and here's the jest, he is in love with my master's sister, Mistress Bridget, and calls her mistress: and there he will sit you a whole afternoon sometimes, reading o' these same abominable, vile – a pox on 'hem, I cannot abide them – rascally verses, poyetry, poyetry, and

speaking of interludes, 'twill make a man burst to hear him. And the wenches, they do so jeer, and ti-he at him – well, should they do so much to me, I'd forswear them all, by the foot of Pharaoh. There's an oath! How many water-bearers shall you hear swear such an oath? Oh, I have a guest. He teaches me. He does swear the legiblest, of any man christened: 'By St. George, the foot of Pharaoh, the body of me, as I am a gentleman and a soldier': such dainty oaths! And withal, he does take this same filthy roguish tobacco, [the finest and cleanliest!] It would do a man good to see the fume come forth at's tonnels! Well, he owes me forty shillings – my wife lent him out of her purse, by sixpence a time – besides his lodging: I would I had it. I shall ha'it, he says, the next Action. Helter skelter, hang sorrow, care'll kill a cat, up-tails all, and a [19][louse for] the hangman.

Scene iv

{A Room in Cob's House}. Bobad{ill} is discovered lying on his bench.

BOBADILL.

Hostess, hostess.

{Enter} Tib.

TIB.

What say you, sir?

BOBADILL.

A cup o' thy small beer, sweet hostess.

TIB.

Sir, there's a gentleman, below, would speak with you.

BOBADILL.

A gentleman! [20]['odso] I am not within.

TIB.

My husband told him you were, sir.

BOBADILL.

What a plague – what meant he?

MATTHEW

{Below} Captain Bobadill?

---

[16] voided
[17] tankard!
[18] tankard
[19] pox on
[20] Godso

BOBADILL.

Who's there? – Take away the basin, good hostess. – Come up, sir.

TIB.

He would desire you to come up, sir. You come into a cleanly house, here.

{*Enter*} *Matthew.*

MATTHEW

[21]['Save you, sir. 'Save you, Captain.]

BOBADILL.

Gentle Master Matthew! Is it you, sir? Please you sit down.

MATTHEW.

Thank you, good Captain, you may see, I am somewhat audacious.

BOBADILL.

Not so, sir. I was requested to supper, last night, by a sort of gallants, where you were wished for, and drunk to, I assure you.

MATTHEW.

Vouchsafe me, by whom, good Captain.

BOBADILL.

Marry, by young Wellbred, and others. Why, hostess, a stool here, for this gentleman.

MATTHEW.

No haste, sir, 'tis very well.

{*Exit Tib.*}

BOBADILL.

Body of me! It was so late ere we parted last night, I can scarce open my eyes, yet; I was but new risen, as you came: how passes the day abroad, sir? You can tell.

MATTHEW.

Faith, some half hour to seven: now trust me, you have an exceeding fine lodging here, very neat, and private!

BOBADILL.

Ay, sir: sit down, I pray you. Master Matthew, in any case, possess no gentleman of our acquaintance, with notice of my lodging.

MATTHEW.

Who? I sir? No.

BOBADILL.

Not that I need to care who know it, for the cabin is convenient, but in regard I would not be too popular, and generally visited, as some are.

MATTHEW.

True, Captain, I conceive you.

BOBADILL.

For, do you see, sir, by the heart of valour, in [22][me] – except it be to some peculiar and choice spirits, to whom I am extraordinarily engaged, as yourself, or so – I could not extend thus far.

MATTHEW.

Oh Lord, [23][sir.] I resolve so.

BOBADILL.

I confess, I love a cleanly and quiet privacy, above all the tumult, and roar of fortune. What new book ha' you there? What! 'Go by, Hieronymo'?

MATTHEW.

Ay, did you ever see it acted? Is't not well penned?

BOBADILL.

Well penned? I would fain see all the poets, of these times, pen such another play as that was! They'll prate and swagger, and keep a stir of art and devices, when, as I am a gentleman, read 'hem, [24]thcy are the most shallow, pitiful, barren fellows, that live upon the face of the earth, again!

MATTHEW.

Indeed, here are a number of fine speeches in this book! 'Oh eyes, no eyes, but fountains fraught with tears'! 'O life, no life, but lively form of death'! Another! 'Oh world, no world, but mass of public wrongs'! A third! 'Confused and filled with murder and misdeeds'! A fourth! Oh, the Muses! Is't not excellent? Is't not simply the best that ever you heard, Captain? Ha? How do you like it?

BOBADILL.

'Tis good.

MATTHEW.

To thee, the purest object to my sense,
The most refined essence heaven covers,
Send I these lines, wherein I do commence
The happy state of turtle-billing lovers.

---

[21] God save you, sir. God save you captain.
[22] myself
[23] sir!
[24] *Insert:* God's so

If they prove rough, unpolished, harsh and rude,
Haste made the waste. Thus, mildly, I conclude.

Bobadill is making him ready all this while.

BOBADILL.
Nay, proceed, proceed. Where's this? [25]

MATTHEW.
This, sir? A toy o' mine own, in my nonage: the infancy of my
Muses! But, when will you come and see my study? Good faith,
I can show you some very good things, I have done of late –
That boot becomes your leg, passing well, Captain, methinks!

BOBADILL.
So, so; it's the fashion, gentlemen now use.

MATTHEW.
[26][Troth,] Captain, an' now you speak o' the fashion, Master
Wellbred's elder brother, and I, are fall'n out exceedingly: this
other day, I happened to enter into some discourse of a hanger,
which I assure you, both for fashion, and workmanship, was
most peremptory-beautiful, and gentleman-like! Yet, he
condemned, and cried it down, for the most pied, and
ridiculous that ever he saw.

BOBADILL.
Squire Downright? The half-brother? Was't not?

MATTHEW.
Ay, sir, he.

BOBADILL.
Hang him, rook, he! Why, he has no more judgement than a
malt-horse. By St. George, I wonder you'd lose a thought upon
such an animal: the most peremptory absurd clown of
Christendom, [this day, he is holden.] I protest to you, as I am a
gentleman, and a soldier, I ne'er changed words, with his like.
By his discourse, he should eat nothing but hay. He was born
for the manger, [pannier, or pack-saddle!] He has not so much
as a good phrase in his belly, but all old iron,[27] and rusty
proverbs! [A good commodity for some smith, to make
hobnails of.]

MATTHEW.
Ay, and he thinks to carry it away with his manhood [still,
where he comes.] He brags he will gi' me the bastinado, as I
hear.

BOBADILL.
How! He the bastinado! How came he by that word, trow?

MATTHEW.
Nay, indeed, he said cudgel me; I termed it so, for my more
grace.

BOBADILL.
That may be: for I was sure, it was none of his word. But,
when? When said he so?

MATTHEW.
Faith, yesterday, they say: a young gallant, a friend of mine told
me so.

BOBADILL.
By the foot of Pharaoh, and 'twere my case now, I should send
him a [28][chartel] presently. The bastinado! A most proper and
sufficient dependence, warranted by the great Caranza. Come
hither. You shall [29][chartel] him. I'll show you a trick, or two,
you shall kill him with, at pleasure: the first stoccata, if you will,
by this air.

MATTHEW.
Indeed, you have absolute knowledge i' the mystery, I have
heard, sir.

BOBADILL.
Of whom? Of whom ha' you heard it, I beseech you?

MATTHEW.
Troth, I have heard it spoken of divers, that you have very rare,
and un-in-one-breath-utter-able-skill, sir.

BOBADILL.
By heaven, no, not I; no skill i' the earth: some small rudiments
i' the science, as to know my time, distance, or so. I have
professed it more for noblemen, and gentlemen's use, than
mine own practice, I assure you. Hostess, accommodate us
with another bed-staff here, quickly.

{*Enter Tib with a puzzled air.*}

Lend us another bed-staff.

{*Exit Tib.*}

The woman does not understand the words of Action. Look
you, sir. Exalt not your point above this state, at any hand, and
let your poniard maintain your defence, thus.

---

[25] *Insert:* Where's this?
[26] Mass,
[27] *Insert:* iron,
[28] challenge
[29] challenge

{Enter Tib with bed-staff.}

Give it to the gentleman, and leave us.

{Exit Tib.}

So, sir. Come on: Oh, twine your body more about, that you may fall to a more sweet comely gentleman-like guard. So, indifferent. Hollow your body more sir, thus. Now, stand fast o' your left leg, note your distance, keep your due proportion of time – Oh, you disorder your point, most irregularly!

MATTHEW.

How is the bearing of it, now, sir?

BOBADILL.

Oh, out of measure ill! A well-experienced hand would pass upon you, at pleasure.

MATTHEW.

How mean you, sir, pass upon me?

BOBADILL.

Why, thus sir. Make a thrust at me. Come in, upon the answer, control your point, and make a full career, at the body. The best-practised gallants of the time, name it the passada: a most desperate thrust, believe it!

MATTHEW.

Well, come, sir.

BOBADILL.

Why, you do not manage your weapon with any facility, or grace to invite me: I have no spirit to play with you. Your dearth of judgement renders you tedious.

MATTHEW.

But one venue, sir.

BOBADILL.

Venue! Fie. Most gross denomination, as ever I heard. Oh, the stoccata, while you live, sir. Note that. Come, put on your cloak, and we'll go to some private place, where you are acquainted, some tavern, or so – and have a bit – I'll send for one of these Fencers, and he shall breath you, by my direction; and, then, I will teach you your trick. You shall kill him with it, at the first, if you please. Why, I will learn you, by the true judgement of the eye, hand, and foot, to control any enemy's point i' the world. Should your adversary confront you with a pistol, 'twere nothing, by this hand, you should, by the same rule, control his bullet, in a line: except it were hail-shot, and spread. What money ha' you about you, Master Matthew?

MATTHEW.

Faith, I ha' not past a two shillings, or so.

BOBADILL.

'Tis somewhat with the least: but, come. We will have a bunch of radish, and salt, to taste our wine; and a pipe of tobacco, to close the orifice of the stomach: and then, we'll call upon young Wellbred. Perhaps we shall meet the Corydon, his brother, there: and put him to the question.

ACT II

Scene i

The Old Jewry. {Kitely's House. Enter} Kitely, Cash {and} Downright.

KITELY.

Thomas, come hither,
There lies a note, within upon my desk,
Here, take my key: it is no matter, neither.
Where is the boy?

CASH.   Within, sir, i' the warehouse.

KITELY.

Let him tell over, straight, that Spanish gold,
And weigh it, with th' pieces of eight. Do you
See the delivery of those silver stuffs,
To Master Lucar. Tell him, if he will,
He shall ha' the grograns, at the rate I told him,
And I will meet him, on the Exchange, anon.

CASH.

Good, sir.

{*Exit Cash.*}

Do you see that fellow, brother Downright?

DOWNRIGHT.

Ay, what of him?

KITELY.   He is a jewel, brother.
I took him up of a child, at my door,
And christened him, gave him mine own name, Thomas,
Since bred him at the Hospital; where proving
A toward imp, I called him home, and taught him
So much, as I have made him my cashier,
And given him, who had none, a surname, Cash:
And find him, in his place so full of faith,
That, I durst trust my life into his hands.

DOWNRIGHT.

So, would not I in any bastard's, brother,
As, it is like, he is: although I knew
Myself his father. But you said you'd somewhat
To tell me, gentle brother, what is't? What is't?

KITELY.

Faith, I am very loath, to utter it,

As fearing, it may hurt your patience:
But, that I know, your judgement is of strength,
Against the nearness of affection –

DOWNRIGHT.

What need this circumstance? Pray you be direct.

KITELY.

I will not say, how much I do ascribe
Unto your friendship; nor, in what regard
I hold your love: but, let my past behaviour,
And usage of your sister, but confirm
How well I've been affected to [your –]

DOWNRIGHT.

You are too tedious, come to the matter, the matter.

KITELY.

Then, without further ceremony, thus.
[30][My] brother Wellbred, sir, I know not how,
Of late, is much declined in what he was,
And greatly altered in his disposition.
When he came first to lodge here in my house,
Ne'er trust me, if I were not proud of him:
Methought he bare himself in such a fashion,
So full of man, and sweetness in his carriage,
And, what was chief, it showed not borrowed in him,
But all he did, became him as his own,
And seemed as perfect, proper, and possessed
As breath, with life, or colour, with the blood.
But, now, his course is so irregular,
So loose, affected, and deprived of grace,
And he himself withal so far fall'n off
From that first place, as scarce no note remains,
To tell men's judgements where he lately stood.
He's grown a stranger to all due respect,
Forgetful of his friends, and not content
To stale himself in all societies,
He makes my house here common, as a mart,
A theatre, a public receptacle
For giddy humour, and diseased riot;
And here, as in a tavern, or a stews,
He, and his wild associates, spend their hours,
In repetition of lascivious jests,
Swear, leap, drink, dance, and revel night by night,
Control my servants: and indeed what not?

---

[30] Our

DOWNRIGHT.

'Sdeins, I know not what I should say to him, i' the whole world! He values me, at a cracked three-farthings, for aught I see: it will never out o' the flesh that's bred i' the bone! I have told him enough, one would think, if that would serve: but counsel to him, is as good, as a shoulder of mutton to a sick horse. Well! He knows what to trust to, for George. Let him spend, and spend, and domineer, till his heart ache; an' he think to be relieved by me, when he is got into one o' your city pounds, [the Counters,] he has the wrong sow by the ear, i' faith: and claps his dish at the wrong man's door. I'll lay my hand o' my halfpenny, ere I part with't, to fetch him out, I'll assure him.

KITELY.

Nay, good brother, let it not trouble you, thus.

DOWNRIGHT.

'Sdeath, he mads me, I could eat my very spur-leathers, for anger! But, why are you so tame? Why do you not speak to him, and tell him how he disquiets your house?

KITELY.

Oh, there are divers reasons to dissuade, brother.
But, would yourself vouchsafe to travail in it,
Though but with plain, and easy circumstance,
It would, both come much better to his sense,
And savour less of stomach, or of passion.
You are his elder brother, and that title
Both gives, and warrants you authority;
Which, by your presence seconded, must breed
A kind of duty in him, and regard:
Whereas, if I should intimate the least,
It would but add contempt, to his neglect,
Heap worse on ill, make up a pile of hatred
That, in the rearing, would come tottering down,
And, in the ruin, bury all our love.
Nay, more than this, brother, if I should speak
He would be ready from his heat of humour,
And overflowing of the vapour, in him,
To blow the ears of his familiars,
With the false breath, of telling, what disgraces,
And low disparagements, I had put upon him.
Whilst they, sir, to relieve him, in the fable,
Make their loose comments, upon every word,
Gesture, or look, I use; mock me all over,
From my flat cap, unto my shining shoes:
And, out of their impetuous rioting fant'sies,
Beget some slander, that shall dwell with me.

And what would that be, think you? Marry, this.
They would give out, because my wife is fair,
Myself but lately married, and my sister
Here sojourning a virgin in my house,
That I were jealous! Nay, as sure as death,
That they would say. And how that I had quarrelled
My brother purposely, thereby to find
An apt pretext, to banish them my house.

DOWNRIGHT.

Mass perhaps so: they're like enough to do it.

KITELY.

Brother, they would, believe it: so should I,
Like one of these penurious quack-salvers,
But set the bills up, to mine own disgrace,
And try experiments upon myself:
Lend scorn and envy, opportunity,
To stab my reputation, and good name –

{Enter} Matthew {and} Bobadill.

MATTHEW.

I will speak to him –

BOBADILL.

Speak to him? Away, by the foot of Pharaoh, you shall not, you shall not do him that grace. The time of day, to you, gentleman o' the house. Is Master Wellbred stirring?

DOWNRIGHT.

How then? What should he do?

BOBADILL.

Gentleman of the house, it is to you: is he within, sir?

KITELY.

He came not to his lodging tonight sir, I assure you.

DOWNRIGHT.

Why, do you hear? You!

BOBADILL.

The gentleman-citizen hath satisfied me, I'll talk to no scavenger.

{Exeunt Matthew and Bobadill.}

DOWNRIGHT.

How, scavenger? Stay sir, stay.

KITELY.

Nay, brother Downright.

DOWNRIGHT.

[31]['Heart!] Stand you away, and you love me.

KITELY.

You shall not follow him now, I pray you, brother, good faith
you shall not: I will overrule you.

DOWNRIGHT.

Ha? Scavenger? Well, go to, I say little: but, by this good day –
God forgive me I should swear – if I put it up so, say, I am the
rankest cow, that ever pissed. 'Sdeins, and I swallow this, I'll
ne'er draw my sword in the sight of Fleet Street again, while I
live: I'll sit in a barn, with madge-howlet, and catch mice first.
Scavenger? ['Heart, and I'll go ne'er to fill that huge tumbrel-
slop of yours, with somewhat, and I have good luck: your
Gargantua breech cannot carry it away so.]

KITELY.

Oh do not fret yourself thus, never think on't.

DOWNRIGHT.

These are my brother's [consorts, these! These are his]
cam'rades, his walking mates! He's a gallant, a cavaliero too,
right hangman cut! Let me not live, and I could not find in my
heart to swinge the whole ging of 'hem, one after another, and
begin with him first. I am grieved, it should be said he is my
brother, and take these courses. Well, as he brews, so he shall
drink, for George, again. Yet, he shall hear on't, and that
tightly too, and I live, i' faith.

KITELY.

But, brother, let your reprehension, then,
Run in an easy current, not o'er high
Carried with rashness, or devouring choler;
But rather use the soft persuading way,
Whose powers will work more gently, and compose
Th'imperfect thoughts you labour to reclaim:
More winning, than enforcing the consent.

DOWNRIGHT.

Ay, ay, let me alone for that, I warrant you.

{Bell rings.}

KITELY.

How now? Oh, the bell rings to breakfast.
Brother, I pray you go in, and bear my wife
Company, till I come; I'll but give order
For some despatch of business to my servants –

{Exit Downright.} Cob passes by with his tankard.

KITELY.

What Cob? Our maids will have you by the back,
I'faith, for coming so late this morning.

COB.

Perhaps so, sir, take heed somebody have not them by the
belly, for walking so late in the evening.

{Exit Cob.}

KITELY.

Well, yet my troubled spirit's somewhat eased,
Though not reposed in that security,
As I could wish: but, I must be content.
Howe'er I set a face on't to the world,
Would I had lost this finger, at a venture,
So Wellbred had ne'er lodged within my house.
Why't cannot be, where there is such resort
Of wanton gallants, and young revellers,
That any woman should be honest long.
Is't like, that factious beauty will preserve
The public weal of chastity, unshaken,
When such strong motives muster, and make head
Against her single peace? No, no. Beware,
When mutual [32][appetite doth meet to treat,]
And spirits of one kind, and quality,
Come once to parley, in the pride of blood:
It is no slow conspiracy, that follows.
Well, to be plain, if I but thought, the time
Had answered their affections: all the world
Should not persuade me, but I were a cuckold.
Marry, I hope, they ha' not got that start:
For opportunity hath baulked 'hem yet,
And shall do still, while I have eyes, and ears
To attend the impositions of my heart.
My presence shall be as an iron bar,
'Twixt the conspiring motions of desire:
Yea, every look, or glance, mine eye ejects,
Shall check occasion, as one doth his slave,
When he forgets the limits of prescription.

{Enter} Dame Kitely {and Bridget.}

DAME KITELY.

Sister Bridget, pray you fetch down the rosewater above in the
closet.

{Exit Bridget.}

---

[31] 'Sblood!
[32] pleasure sways the appetite,

Sweetheart, will you come in, to breakfast?

KITELY.
{*Aside.*} An' she have overheard me now?

DAME KITELY.
I pray thee, good muss, we stay for you.

KITELY.
{*Aside.*} By [33][heaven] I would not for a thousand [34][angels!]

DAME KITELY.
What ail you sweetheart, are you not well? Speak good muss.

KITELY.
Troth, my head aches extremely, on a sudden.

DAME KITELY.
{*Putting her hand to his forehead*} Oh, [35][the Lord!]

KITELY.
How now? What?

DAME KITELY.
[36][Alas,] how it burns! Muss, keep you warm, good truth it is this new disease! There's a number are troubled withal! For love's sake, sweetheart, come in, out of the air.

KITELY.
{*Aside*} How simple, and how subtle are her answers!
A new disease, and many troubled with it!
Why, true: she heard me, all the world to nothing.

DAME KITELY.
I pray thee, good sweetheart, come in; the air will do you harm, in troth.

KITELY.
{*Aside*} The air! She has me i' the wind!
Sweetheart! – I'll come to you presently: 'twill away, I hope.

DAME KITELY.
Pray [37][heaven] it do.

{*Exit Dame Kitely.*}

KITELY.
A new disease? I know not, new, or old,
But it may well be called poor mortals' plague:
For, like a pestilence, it doth infect
The houses of the brain. First, it begins
Solely to work upon the fantasy,
Filling her seat with such pestiferous air,
As soon corrupts the judgement; and from thence
Sends like contagion to the memory:

Still each to other giving the infection.
Which, as a subtle vapour, spreads itself,
Confusedly, through every sensive part,
Till not a thought, or motion, in the mind,
Be free from the black poison of suspect.
Ah, but what misery' is it, to know this?
Or, knowing it, to want the mind's erection,
In such extremes? Well, I will once more strive,
[38][In spite of this black cloud,] myself to be,
And shake the fever off, that thus shakes me.

{*Exit.*}

Scene ii

{*Moorfields. Enter*} Brainworm {*like a maimed sub-officer.*}

BRAINWORM.
[39]['Slid,] I cannot choose but laugh, to see myself translated thus, from a poor creature to a creator; for now must I create an intolerable sort of lies, or my present profession loses the grace: [and yet the lie to a man of my coat, is as ominous a fruit, as the fico.] Oh sir, it holds for good polity ever, to have that outwardly in vilest estimation, that inwardly is most dear to us. So much, for my borrowed shape. Well, the troth is, my old master intends to follow my young, dry foot, over Moorfields, to London, this morning: now I, knowing, of this hunting-match, or rather conspiracy, and to insinuate with my young master [– for so must we that are blue-waiters, and men of hope and service do, or perhaps we may wear motely at the year's end, and who wears motley, you know –] have got me afore, in this disguise, determining here to lie in ambuscado, and intercept him, in the mid-way. If I can but get his cloak, his purse, his hat, nay, anything, to cut him off, that is, to say his journey, veni, vidi, vici, I may say with Captain Caesar, I am made for ever, i' faith. Well, now must I practise to get the true garb of one of these lance-knights, my arm here, and my – young master! And his cousin, Master Stephen, as I am true counterfeit man of war, and no soldier!

---

[33] Christ
[34] crowns!
[35] Jesu!
[36] Good Lord,
[37] God
[38] Even in despite of hell,
[39] 'Sblood,

Brainworm {moves away. Enter} Ed. Kno'well {and} Stephen.

ED. KNO'WELL.
So sir, and how then, coz?

STEPHEN.
[40]['Sfoot,] I have lost my purse, I think.

ED. KNO'WELL.
How? Lost your purse? Where? When had you it?

STEPHEN.
I cannot tell. Stay?

BRAINWORM.
{*Aside*} 'Slid, I am afeared, they will know me, would I could get by them.

ED. KNO'WELL.
What? Ha' you it?

STEPHEN.
No, I think I was bewitched, I –

ED. KNO'WELL.
Nay, do not weep the loss,[41] hang it, let it go.

STEPHEN.
Oh, it's here: no, and it had been lost, I had not cared, but for a jet ring Mistress Mary sent me.

ED. KNO'WELL.
A jet ring? Oh, the poesy, the poesy?

STEPHEN.
Fine, i'faith! 'Though fancy sleep, my love is deep.' Meaning that though I did not fancy her, yet she loved me deeply.

ED. KNO'WELL.
Most excellent!

STEPHEN.
And then, I sent her another and my poesy was: 'The deeper, the sweeter, I'll be judged by St. Peter.'

ED. KNO'WELL.
How, by St. Peter? I do not conceive that!

STEPHEN.
Marry, St. Peter, to make up the metre.

[ED. KNO'WELL.
Well, there the saint was your good patron, he helped you at your need: thank him, thank him.]

BRAINWORM.
{*Aside*} I cannot take leave on 'hem, so: I will venture, come what will. {*Goes towards them.*} Gentlemen, please you change a few crowns, for a very excellent good blade, here? I am a poor gentleman, a soldier, one that, in the better state of my fortunes, scorned so mean a refuge, but now it is the humour of necessity, to have it so. You seem to be gentlemen, well affected to martial men, else I should rather die with silence, than live with shame: however, vouchsafe to remember, it is my want speaks, not myself. This condition agrees not with my spirit –

ED. KNO'WELL.
Where hast thou served?

BRAINWORM.
May it please you, sir, in all the late wars of Bohemia, Hungaria, Dalmatia, Poland, where not, sir? I have been a poor servitor, by sea and land, any time this fourteen years, and followed the fortunes of the best commanders in Christendom. I was twice shot at the taking of Aleppo, once at the relief of Vienna; I have been at [42] Marseilles, Naples, and the Adriatic gulf, a gentleman-slave in the galleys, thrice, where I was most dangerously shot in the head, through both the thighs, and yet, being thus maimed, I am void of maintenance, nothing left me but my scars, the noted marks of my resolution.

STEPHEN.
How will you sell this rapier, friend?

BRAINWORM.
Generous sir, I refer it to your own judgement; you are a gentleman, give me what you please.

STEPHEN.
True, I am a gentleman, I know that friend: but what though? I pray you say, what would you ask?

BRAINWORM.
I assure you, the blade may become the side, or thigh of the best prince, in Europe.

ED. KNO'WELL.
Ay, with a velvet scabbard, I think.

STEPHEN.
Nay, and't be mine it shall have a velvet scabbard, coz, that's flat: I'd not wer it as 'tis, and you would give me an angel.

---

[40] God's foot
[41] *Insert:* a pox on it,
[42] *Insert:* America

BRAINWORM.

At your worship's pleasure, sir: nay, 'tis a most pure Toledo.

STEPHEN.

I had rather it were a Spaniard! But tell me, what shall I give you for it? An' it had a silver hilt –

ED. KNO'WELL.

Come, come, you shall not buy it; hold, there's a shilling fellow, take thy rapier.

STEPHEN.

Why, but I will buy it now, because you say so, and there's another shilling, fellow. I scorn to be outbidden. What, shall I walk with a cudgel, [like Higginbottom?] And may have a rapier, for money?

ED. KNO'WELL.

You may buy one in the city.

STEPHEN.

Tut, I'll buy this i' the field, so I will, I have a mind to't, because 'tis a field rapier. Tell me your lowest price.

ED. KNO'WELL.

You shall not buy it, I say.

STEPHEN.

By this money, but I will, though I give more than 'tis worth.

ED. KNO'WELL.

Come away, you are a fool.

STEPHEN.

Friend, I am a fool, that's granted: but I'll have it, for that word's sake. Follow me, for your money.

BRAINWORM.

At your service, sir.

{*Exeunt.*}

Scene iii

{*Another part of Moorfields. Enter*} Kno'well.

KNO'WELL.

I cannot lose the thought, yet, of this letter,
Sent to my son: nor leave t'admire the change
Of manners, and the breeding of our youth,
Within the kingdom, since myself was one.
When I was young, he lived not in the stews,

Durst have conceived a scorn, and uttered it,
On a grey head; [age was authority
Against a buffoon:] and a man had, then,
A certain reverence paid unto his years,
[That had none due unto his life. So much
The sanctity of some prevailed, for others.]
But, now, we all are fall'n; youth, from their fear:
And age, from that, which bred it, good example.
Nay, would ourselves were not the first, even parents,
That did destroy the hopes, in our own children:
[Or they not learned our vices, in their cradles,
And sucked][43] in our ill customs, with their milk.
Ere all their teeth be born, or they can speak,
We make their palates cunning! The first words,
We form their tongues with, are licentious jests!
Can it call, whore? Cry, bastard? Oh, then, kiss it,
A witty child! Can't swear? The father's dearling!
Give it two plums. Nay, rather than't shall learn
No bawdy song, the mother' herself will teach it!
But, this is in the infancy; the days
Of the long coat: when it puts on the breeches,
It will put off all this. Ay, it is like:
When it is gone into the bone already.
No, no: this dye goes deeper than the coat,
Or shirt, or skin. It stains, unto the liver,
And heart, in some. And, rather, than it should not,
Note, what we fathers do! Look, how we live!
What mistresses we keep! At what expense,
In our son's eyes! Where they may handle our gifts,
Hear our lascivious courtships, see our dalliance,
Taste of the same provoking meats, with us,
To ruin of our states! Nay, when our own
Portion is fled, to prey on their remainder,
We call them into fellowship of vice!
Bait 'hem with the young chambermaid, to seal!
[And teach 'hem all bad ways, to buy affliction!]
This is one path! But there are millions more,
[In which we spoil our own, with leading them.]
Well, I thank heaven, I never yet was he,
That travelled with my son, before sixteen,
To show him, the Venetian courtesans.
Nor read the grammar of cheating, I had made
To my sharp boy, at twelve: repeating still
The rule, 'Get money'; still, 'get money, boy;
No matter by what means; money will do
More, boy, than my lord's letter'. Neither have I

---

[43] Who suck

Dressed snails, or mushrooms curiously before him,
Perfumed my sauces, [and taught him to make 'hem;
Preceding still, with my grey gluttony,
At all the ordinaries:][44]and only feared
His palate should degenerate, not his manners.
These are the trade of fathers, now! However
My son, I hope, hath met within my threshold,
None of these household precedents; which are strong,
And swift, to rape youth, to their precipice.
But, let the house at home be ne'er so clean –
[Swept, or kept sweet from filth; nay, dust, and cobwebs:]
If he will live, abroad, with his companions,
In dung, and leystalls; it is worth a fear.
[Nor is the danger of conversing less,
Than all that I have mentioned of example.]

{Enter} Brainworm {disguised as before.}

BRAINWORM.
  {Aside} My master! Nay, faith have at you: I am fleshed now, I
  have sped so well. – Worshipful sir, I beseech you, respect the
  estate of a poor soldier; I am ashamed of this base course of life –
  God's my comfort – but extremity provokes me to't, what
  remedy?

KNO'WELL.
  I have not for you, now.

BRAINWORM.
  By the faith I bear unto truth, gentleman, it is no ordinary
  custom in me, but only to preserve manhood. I protest to you, a
  man I have been, a man I may be, by your sweet bounty.

KNO'WELL.
  'Pray thee, good friend, be satisfied.

BRAINWORM.
  Good sir, by [45][that hand,] you may do the part of a kind
  gentleman, in lending a poor soldier the price of two cans of
  beer – a matter of small value. The king of heaven shall pay you,
  and I shall rest thankful: sweet worship –

KNO'WELL.
  Nay, and you be so importunate –

BRAINWORM.
  Oh, tender sir, need will have this course: I was not made to this
  vile use! Well, the edge of the enemy could not have abated me
  so much; it's hard when a man hath served in his prince's cause,
  and be thus – (*He weeps.*) Honourable worship, let me derive a
  small piece of silver from you, it shall not be given in the course
  of time, by this good ground, I was fain to pawn my rapier last
  night for a poor supper, I had sucked the hilts long before, I am
  a pagan else: sweet honour.

KNO'WELL.
  Believe me, I am taken with some wonder,
  To think, a fellow of thy outward presence
  Should, in the frame, and fashion of his mind,
  Be so degenerate, and sordid-base!
  Art thou a man? And sham'st thou not to beg?
  To practise such a servile kind of life?
  Why, were thy education ne'er so mean,
  Having thy limbs, a thousand fairer courses
  Offer themselves, to thy election.
  Either the wars might still supply thy wants,
  Or service of some virtuous gentleman,
  Or honest labour: nay, what can I name,
  But would become thee better than to beg?
  But men of thy condition feed on sloth,
  As doth the beetle, on the dung she breeds in,
  Not caring how the mettle of your minds
  Is eaten with the rust of idleness.
  Now, afore [46][me], whate'er he be, that should
  Relieve a person of thy quality,
  While thou insist'st in this loose desperate course,
  I would esteem the sin, not thine, but his.

BRAINWORM.
  Faith sir, I would gladly find some other course, if so –

KNO'WELL.
  Ay, you'd gladly find it, but you will not seek it.

BRAINWORM.
  Alas sir, where should a man seek? In the wars, there's no
  ascent by desert in these days, but – and for service, would it
  were as soon purchased, as wished for. The air's my comfort. I
  know, what I would say –

KNO'WELL.
  What's thy name?

BRAINWORM.
  Please you, Fitzsword, sir.

KNO'WELL.   Fitzsword?
  Say, that a man should entertain thee now,
  Wouldst thou be honest, humble, just, and true?

---

44 Yea,
45 Jesu
46 God

BRAINWORM.

    Sir, by the place, and honour of a soldier –

KNO'WELL.

    Nay, nay, I like not these affected oaths;
    Speak plainly man: what thinkst thou of my words?

BRAINWORM.

    Nothing, sir, but wish my fortunes were as happy, as my
    service should be honest.

KNO'WELL.

    Well, follow me, I'll prove thee, if thy deeds
    Will carry a proportion to thy words.

BRAINWORM.

    Yes sir, straight, I'll but garter my hose.

                                {Exit Kno'well.}

[Oh that my belly were hooped now, for I am ready to burst
with laughing! Never was bottle, or bagpipe fuller.] 'Slid, was
there ever seen a fox in years to betray himself thus? Now shall I
be possessed of all his counsels: and, by that conduit, my young
master. Well, he is resolved to prove my honesty; faith, and I
am resolved to prove his patience: Oh I shall abuse him
intolerably. This small piece of service, will bring him clean out
of love with the soldier, forever. [He will never come within the
sign of it, the sight of a cassock, or a musket-rest again.] He will
hate the musters at Mile End for it, to his dying day. It's no
matter, let the world think me a bad counterfeit, if I cannot give
him the slip, at an instant: [why, this is better than to have
stayed his journey!] Well, I'll follow him: Oh, how I long to be
employed.

                                          {Exit.}

ACT THREE

Scene i

*{The Old Jewry. A Room in the Windmill Tavern. Enter} Matthew,
Wellbred {and} Bobadill.*

MATTHEW.

    Yes faith, sir, we were at your lodging to seek you, too.

WELLBRED.

    Oh, I came not there tonight.

BOBADILL.

    Your brother delivered us as much.

WELLBRED.

    Who? My brother Downright?

BOBADILL.

    He. Master Wellbred, I know not in what kind you hold me,
    but let me say to you this: as sure as honour, I esteem it so much
    out of the sunshine of reputation, to throw the least beam of
    regard, upon such a –[47]

WELLBRED.

    Sir, I must hear no ill words of my brother.

BOBADILL.

    I, protest to you, as I have a thing to be saved about me, I never
    saw any gentleman-like part –

WELLBRED.

    Good Captain, faces about, to some other discourse.

BOBADILL.

    With your leave, sir, and there were no more men living upon
    the face of the earth, I should not fancy him, by St. George.

MATTHEW.

    Troth, nor I, he is of a rustical cut, I know not how: he doth not
    carry himself like a gentleman of fashion –

WELLBRED.

    Oh, Master Matthew, that's a grace peculiar but to a few; *quos
    aequus amavit Jupiter.*

MATTHEW.

    I understand you sir.

---

[47] *Insert:* a dunghill of flesh.

WELLBRED.

No question, you do, or you do not, sir.

Young Kno'well enters {with Stephen}.

Ned Kno'well! By my soul welcome; how dost thou sweet spirit, my genius. 'Slid I shall love Apollo, and the mad Thespian girls the better, while I live, for this; my dear fury: now, I see there's some love in thee! Sirrah, these be the two I writ to thee of. Nay, what a drowsy humour is this now? Why dost thou not speak?

ED. KNO'WELL.

Oh, you are a fine gallant, you sent me a rare letter!

WELLBRED.

Why, was't not rare?

ED. KNO'WELL.

Yes, I'll be sworn, I was ne'er guilty of reading the like; match it in all Pliny, or Symmachus's epistles, and I'll have my judgement burned in the ear for a rogue: make much of thy vein, for it is inimitable. But I marle what camel it was, that had the carriage of it, for doubtless, he was no ordinary beast, that brought it!

WELLBRED.

Why?   .

ED. KNO'WELL.

Why, sayst thou? Why dost thou think that any reasonable creature, especially in the morning – the sober time of the day too – could have mista'en my father for me?

WELLBRED.

[48]['Slid], you jest, I hope?

ED. KNO'WELL.

Indeed, the best use we can turn it to, is to make a jest on't, now: but I'll assure you, my father had the full view o' your flourishing style, some hour before I saw it.

WELLBRED.

What a dull slave was this! But, sirrah, what said he to it, i' faith?

ED. KNO'WELL.

Nay, I know not what he said: but I have a shrewd guess what he thought.

WELLBRED.

What? What?

ED. KNO'WELL.

Marry, that thou art some strange dissolute young fellow, and I a grain or two better, for keeping thee company.

WELLBRED.

Tut, that thought is like the moon in her last quarter, 'twill change shortly: but sirrah, I pray thee be acquainted with my two [49][hang-byes] here; thou wilt take exceeding pleasure in 'hem if thou hear'st 'hem once go: my wind instruments. I'll wind 'hem up – but what strange piece of silence is this? The sign of the dumb man?

ED. KNO'WELL.

Oh, sir, a kinsman of mine, one that may make your music the fuller, and he please, he has his humour, sir.

WELLBRED.

Oh, what is't? What is't?

ED. KNO'WELL.

Nay, I'll neither do your judgement, nor his folly that wrong, as to prepare your apprehension: I'll leave him to the mercy o'your search, if you can take him, so.

WELLBRED.

Well, Captain Bobadill, Master Matthew, pray you know this gentleman here, he is a friend of mine, and one that will deserve your affection. (*To Master Stephen*:) I know not your name sir, but I shall be glad of any occasion, to render me more familiar to you.

STEPHEN.

My name is Master Stephen, sir, I am this gentleman's own cousin, sir, his father is mine uncle, sir, I am somewhat melancholy, but you shall command me, sir, in whatsoever is incident to a gentleman.

BOBADILL.

(*To {Ed.} Kno'well*:) Sir, I must tell you this, I am no general man, but for Master Wellbred's sake – you may embrace it, at what height of favour you please – I do communicate with you: and conceive you, to be a gentleman of some parts, I love few words.

ED. KNO'WELL.

And I fewer, sir. I have scarce enow, to thank you.

MATTHEW.

(*To Master Stephen*:) But are you indeed, sir? So given to it?

---

[48] 'Sblood
[49] zanies

STEPHEN.
Ay, truly, sir, I am mightily given to melancholy.

MATTHEW.
Oh, it's [50][only your] fine humour, sir, your true melancholy breeds you perfect fine wit, sir: I am melancholy myself divers times, sir, and then do I no more but take pen, and paper presently, and overflow you half a score, or a dozen of sonnets, at a sitting.

ED. KNO'WELL.
(*Aside*) Sure, he utters them then, by the gross.

STEPHEN.
Truly sir, and I love such things, out of measure.

ED. KNO'WELL.
I' faith, better than in measure, I'll undertake.

MATTHEW.
Why, I pray you, sir, make use of my study, it's at your service.

STEPHEN.
I thank you sir, I shall be bold, I warrant you; have you a stool there, to be melancholy upon?

MATTHEW.
That I have, sir, and some papers there of mine own doing, at idle hours, that you'll say there's some sparks of wit in 'hem, when you see them.

WELLBRED.
{*Aside*} Would the sparks would kindle once, and become a fire amongst 'hem, I might see self-love burnt for her heresy.

STEPHEN.
Cousin, is it well? Am I melancholy enough?

ED. KNO'WELL.
Oh ay, excellent!

WELLBRED.
Captain Bobadill: why muse you so?

ED. KNO'WELL.
He is melancholy, too.

BOBADILL.
Faith, sir, I was thinking of a most honourable piece of service, was performed tomorrow, being St. Mark's day: shall be some ten years, now.

ED. KNO'WELL.
In what place, Captain?

BOBADILL.
Why, at the beleag'ring of Strigonium, where, in less than two hours, seven hundred resolute gentlemen, as any were in Europe, lost their lives upon the breach. I'll tell you, gentlemen, it was the first, but the best leager, that ever I beheld, with these eyes, except the taking in of – what do you call it, last year, by the Genoways? – but that, of all other, was the most fatal, and dangerous exploit, that ever I was ranged in, since I first bore arms before the face of the enemy, as I am a gentleman, and soldier.

STEPHEN.
'So, I had as lief, as an angel, I could swear as well as that gentleman!

ED. KNO'WELL.
Then, you were a servitor, at both it seems! At Strigonium? And what-you-call't?

BOBADILL.
Oh Lord, sir! By St. George, I was the first man, that entered the breach: and, had I not effected it with resolution, I had been slain, if I had had a million of lives.

ED. KNO'WELL.
'Twas pity, you had not ten; a cat's, and your own, i' faith. But, was it possible?

MATTHEW.
{*Aside to Stephen*:} 'Pray you, mark this discourse, sir.

STEPHEN.
{*To Matthew*:} So, I do.

BOBADILL.
I assure you, upon my reputation, 'tis true, and yourself shall confess.

ED. KNO'WELL.
You must bring me to the rack, first.

BOBADILL.
Observe me judicially, sweet sir, they had planted me three demi-culverins, just in the mouth of the breach; now, sir, as we were to give on, their master-gunner – a man of no mean skill, and mark, you must think – confronts me with his linstock, ready to give fire; I spying his intendment, discharged my petrionel in his bosom, and with these single arms, my poor rapier, ran violently, upon the Moors, that guarded the ordnance, and put 'hem pell-mell to the sword.

---

[50] your only

WELLBRED.
>To the sword? To the rapier, Captain.

ED. KNO'WELL.
>Oh, it was a good figure observed, sir! But did you all this, Captain, without hurting your blade?

BOBADILL.
>Without any impeach, o' the earth: you shall perceive sir. It is the most fortunate weapon, that ever rid on gentleman's thigh: shall I tell you, sir? You talk of Morglay, Excalibur, Durindana, or so? Tut, I lend no credit to that is fabled of 'hem, I know the virtue of mine own, and therefore I dare, the boldlier, maintain it.

STEPHEN.
>I marle whether it be a Toledo, or no?

BOBADILL.
>A most perfect Toledo, I assure you, sir.

STEPHEN.
>I have a countryman of his, here.

MATTHEW.
>Pray you, let's see, sir: yes faith, it is!

BOBADILL.
>This a Toledo? Pish.

STEPHEN.
>Why do you pish, Captain?

BOBADILL.
>A Fleming, by heaven, I'll buy them for a guilder, apiece, an' I would have a thousand of them.

ED. KNO'WELL.
>How say you, cousin? I told you thus much.

WELLBRED.
>Where bought you it, Master Stephen?

STEPHEN.
>Of a scurvy rogue soldier – a hundred of lice go with him! He swore it was a Toledo.

BOBADILL.
>A poor provant rapier, no better.

MATTHEW.
>51[Man], I think it be, indeed, now I look on't, better.

ED. KNO'WELL.
>Nay, the longer you look on't, the worse. Put it up, put it up.

STEPHEN.
>Well, I will put it up, but by – {*Aside*} I ha' forgot the Captain's oath, I thought to ha' sworn by it – an' ere I meet him –

WELLBRED.
>Oh, it is past help now, sir, you must have patience.

STEPHEN.
>Whoreson coney-catching rascal! I could eat the very hilts for anger!

ED. KNO'WELL.
>A sign of good digestion! You have an ostrich stomach, cousin.

STEPHEN.
>A stomach? Would I had him here, you should see, an' I had a stomach.

WELLBRED.
>It's better as 'tis: come, gentlemen, shall we go?

>{*Enter*} Brainworm {*disguised as before.*}

ED. KNO'WELL.
>A miracle, cousin, look here! Look here!

STEPHEN.
>Oh, God's lid, by your leave, do you know me, sir?

BRAINWORM.
>Ay sir, I know you, by sight.

STEPHEN.
>You sold me a rapier, did you not?

BRAINWORM.
>Yes, marry, did I sir.

STEPHEN.
>You said, it was a Toledo, ha?

BRAINWORM.
>True, I did so.

STEPHEN.
>But, it is none?

BRAINWORM.
>No sir, I confess, it is none.

STEPHEN.
>Do you confess it? Gentlemen, bear witness, he has confessed it. By God's will, and you had not confessed it –

---

51 Mass

ED. KNO'WELL.
Oh cousin, forbear, forbear.

STEPHEN.
Nay, I have done, cousin.

WELLBRED.
Why, you have done like a gentleman, he has confessed it, what would you more?

STEPHEN.
Yes, by his leave, he is a rascal, under his favour, do you see?

ED. KNO'WELL.
{*Aside to Wellbred*:} [Ay, by his leave, he is, and under favour: a pretty piece of civility!] Sirrah, how dost thou like him?

WELLBRED.
[Oh, it's a most precious fool, make much on him:] I can compare him to nothing more happily, than a drum; for everyone may play upon him.

ED. KNO'WELL.
With me, sir? You have not another Toledo to sell, ha' you?

BRAINWORM.
You are conceited, sir, your name is Master Kno'well, as I take it?

ED. KNO'WELL.
You are i' the right; you mean not to proceed in the catechism, do you?

BRAINWORM.
No sir, I am none of that coat.

ED. KNO'WELL.
Of as bare a coat, though; well, say sir.

BRAINWORM.
Faith, sir, I am but servant to the drum extraordinary, and indeed, this smoky varnish being washed off, and three or four patches removed, I appear your worship's in reversion, after the decease of your good father, Brainworm.

ED. KNO'WELL.
Brainworm! 'Slight, what breath of a conjurer, hath blown thee hither in this shape?

BRAINWORM.
The breath o' your letter, sir, this morning: the same that blew you to the Windmill, and your father after you.

ED. KNO'WELL.
My father?

BRAINWORM.
Nay, never start, 'tis true, he has followed you over the fields, by the foot, as you would do a hare i' the snow.

ED. KNO'WELL.
Sirrah, Wellbred, what shall we do sirrah? My father is come over, after me.

WELLBRED.
Thy father? Where is he?

BRAINWORM.
At Justice Clement's house here, in Coleman Street, where he but stays my return; and then –

WELLBRED.
Who's this? Brainworm?

BRAINWORM.
The same, sir.

WELLBRED.
Why how, i' the name of wit, com'st thou transmuted, thus?

BRAINWORM.
Faith, a device, a device: nay, for the love of [52][reason], gentlemen, and avoiding the danger, stand not here, withdraw, and I'll tell you all.

WELLBRED.
But, art thou sure, he will stay thy return?

BRAINWORM.
Do I live, sir? What a question is that?

WELLBRED.
We'll prorogue his expectation then, a little: Brainworm, thou shalt go with us. Come on, gentlemen, nay, I pray thee, sweet Ned, droop not: 'heart, and our wits be so wretchedly dull, that one old plodding brain can outstrip us all, [53][would we were e'en pressed, to make porters of; and serve out the remnant of our days, in Thames Street, or at Custom House quay, in a civil war, against the carmen.]

BRAINWORM.
Amen, amen, amen, say I.

{*Exeunt.*}

---

[52] God
[53] Lord, I beseech thee, may we lie and starve in some miserable spittle, where we may never see the face of any true spirit again, but be perpetually haunted with some church-yard hobgoblin in *seculo seculorum*.

Scene ii

{The Old Jewry. Kitely's Warehouse. Enter} Kitely {and} Cash.

KITELY.
What says he, Thomas? Did you speak with him?

CASH.
He says he will expect you, sir, within this half hour.

KITELY.
Has he the money ready, can you tell?

CASH.
Yes, sir, the money was brought in, last night.

KITELY.
Oh, that's well: fetch me my cloak, my cloak.

{Exit Cash.}

Stay, let me see, an hour, to go and come;
Ay, that will be the least: and then 'twill be
An hour, before I can dispatch with him;
Or very near: well, I will say two hours.
Two hours? Ha? Things, never dreamed of yet,
May be contrived, ay, and effected too,
In two hours' absence: well, I will not go.
Two hours; no, fleering opportunity,
I will not give your subtlety that scope.
Who will not judge him worthy to be robbed,
That sets his doors wide open to a thief,
And shows the felon, where his treasure lies?
Again, what earthy spirit but will attempt
To taste the fruit of beauty's golden tree,
When leaden sleep seals up the dragon's eyes?
I will not go. Business, go by, for once.
No, beauty, no; you are of too good caract,
To be left so, without a guard, or open!
Your lustre too'll inflame, at any distance,
Draw courtship to you, as a jet doth straws,
Put motion in a stone, strike fire from ice,
Nay, make a porter leap you, with his burden!
You must be then kept up, close, and well-watched,
For, give you opportunity, no quicksand
Devours, or swallows swifter! He that lends
His wife, if she be fair, or time, or place;
Compels her to be false. I will not go.
The dangers are too many. And, then, the dressing
Is a most main attractive! Our great heads,
Within the city, never were in safety,
Since our wives wore these little caps: I'll change 'hem,

I'll change 'hem, straight, in mine. Mine shall no more
Wear three-piled acorns to make my horns ache.
Nor will I go, I am resolved for that.

{Enter Cash, with cloak.}

Carry' in my cloak again. Yet, stay. Yet, do too.
I will defer going, on all occasions.

CASH.
Sir. Snare, your scrivener, will be there with th' bonds.

KITELY.
That's true! Fool on me! I had clean forgot it,
I must go. What's a clock?

CASH: Exchange time, sir.

KITELY.
{Aside} 'Heart, then will Wellbred presently be here, too,
With one, or other of his loose consorts.
I am a knave, if I know what to say,
What course to take, or which way to resolve.
My brain, methinks, is like an hour-glass,
Wherein, my' imaginations run, like sands,
Filling up time; but then are turned, and turned:
So, that I know not what to stay upon,
And less, to put in act. It shall be so.
Nay, I dare build upon his secrecy,
He knows not to deceive. – Thomas!

CASH.   Sir.

KITELY.
{Aside} Yet not, I have bethought me, too, I will not. –
Thomas, is Cob within?

CASH.   I think he be, sir.

KITELY.
{Aside} But he'll prate too, there's no speech of him.
No, there were no man o' the earth to Thomas,
If I durst trust him; there is all the doubt.
But, should he have a chink in him, I were gone,
Lost i' my fame for ever: talk for th' Exchange.
The manner he hath stood with, till this present,
Doth promise no such change! What should I fear then?
Well, come what will, I'll tempt my fortune, once. –
Thomas – you may deceive me, but, I hope –
Your love, to me, is more –

CASH.   Sir, if a servant's
Duty, with faith, may be called love, you are
More than in hope, you are possessed of it.

KITELY.
    I thank you, heartily, Thomas; gi' me your hand:
    With all my heart, Good Thomas. I have, Thomas,
    A secret to impart, unto you – but
    When once you have it, I must seal your lips up:
    So far, I tell you, Thomas.

CASH.   Sir, for that –

KITELY.
    Nay, hear me, out. Think, I esteem you, Thomas,
    When, I will let you in, thus, to my private.
    It is a thing sits, nearer, to my crest,
    Than thou art ware of, Thomas. If thou should'st
    Reveal it, but –

CASH.   How? I reveal it?

KITELY.   Nay,
    I do not think thou would'st; but if thou should'st:
    'Twere a great weakness.

CASH.   A great treachery.
    Give it no other name.

KITELY.   Thou wilt not do't, then?

CASH.
    Sir, if I do, mankind disclaim me, ever.

KITELY.
    {*Aside*} He will not swear, he has some reservation,
    Some concealed purpose, and close meaning, sure:
    Else, being urged so much, how should he choose,
    But lend an oath to all this protestation?
    He's no [54][precisian], that I am certain of.
    Nor rigid Roman Catholic. He'll play,
    At fayles, and tick-tack, I have heard him swear.
    What should I think of it? Urge him again,
    And by some other [55][say?] I will do so. –
    Well, Thomas, thou hast sworn not to disclose;
    Yes, you did swear?

CASH.   Not yet, sir, but I will,
    Please you –

KITELY.
    No, Thomas, I dare take thy word.
    But; if thou wilt swear, do, as thou think'st good;
    I am resolved without it; at thy pleasure.

CASH.
    By my soul's safety then, sir, I protest.
    My tongue shall ne'er take knowledge of a word,

    Delivered me in nature of your trust.

KITELY.
    It's too much, these ceremonies need not,
    I know thy faith to be as firm as rock.
    Thomas, come hither, near: we cannot be
    Too private, in this business. So it is –
    {*Aside*} Now, he has sworn, I dare the safelier venture –
    I have of late, by divers observations –
    {*Aside*} But whether his oath can bind him, yea, or no;
    Being not taken lawfully? Ha? Say you?
    I will ask counsel, ere I do proceed –
    Thomas, it will be now too late to stay,
    I'll spy some fitter time soon, or tomorrow.

CASH.
    Sir at your pleasure?

KITELY.   I will think. And, Thomas,
    I pray you search the books 'gainst my return,
    For the receipts 'twixt me, and Traps.

CASH.   I will, sir.

KITELY.
    And, hear you, if your mistress' brother, Wellbred,
    Chance to bring hither any gentlemen,
    Ere I come back; let one straight bring me word.

CASH.
    Very well, sir.

KITELY.   To the Exchange; do you hear?
    Or here in Coleman Street, to Justice Clement's.
    Forget it not, nor be not out of the way.

CASH.
    I will not, sir.

KITELY.   I pray you have a care on't.
    Or whether he come, or no, if any other,
    Stranger, or else, fail not to send me word.

CASH.
    I shall not, sir.

KITELY.   Be't your special business
    Now, to remember it.

CASH.   Sir. I warrant you.

---

[54] puritan
[55] way?

KITELY.

But, Thomas, this is not the secret, Thomas,
I told you of.

CASH.   No, sir. I do suppose it.

KITELY.

Believe me, it is not.

CASH.   Sir. I do believe you.

KITELY.

By heaven, it is not, that's enough. But, Thomas,
I would not, you should utter it, do you see?
To any creature living, yet, I care not.
Well, I must hence. Thomas, conceive this much.
It was a trial of you, when I meant
So deep a secret to you, I mean not this,
But that I have to tell you, this is nothing, this.
But, Thomas, keep this from my wife, I charge you,
Locked up in silence, midnight, buried here.
{*Aside.*} No greater hell, than to be slave to fear.

                                        {*Exit.*}

CASH.

'Locked up in silence, midnight, buried here'.
Whence should this flood of passion, trow, take head? Ha?
Best, dream no longer of this running humour,
For fear I sink! The violence of the stream
Already hath transported me so far,
That I can feel no ground at all! But soft,
Oh, 'tis our water-bearer: somewhat has crossed him, now.

{*Enter*} Cob.

COB.

Fasting days? What would you tell me of fasting days? 'Slid,
would they were all on a light fire for me: they say, the whole
world shall be consumed with fire one day, but would I had
these ember-weeks, and villainous Fridays burnt, in the
meantime, and then –

CASH.

Why, how now Cob, what moves thee to this choler? Ha?

COB.

Collar, Master Thomas? I scorn your collar, ay sir, I am none
o' your cart-horse, though I carry, and draw water. An' you
offer to ride me, with your collar, or halter either, I may hap
show you a jade's trick, sir.

CASH.

Oh, you'll slip your head out of the collar? Why, goodman Cob,

you mistake me.

COB.

Nay, I have my rheum, and I can be angry as well as another,
sir.

CASH.

Thy rheum, Cob? Thy humour, thy humour? Thou mistak'st.

COB.

Humour? Mack, I think it be so, indeed: what is that humour?
Some rare thing, I warrant.

CASH.

Marry, I'll tell thee, Cob: it is a gentleman-like monster, bred,
in the special gallantry of our time, by affectation; and fed by
folly.

COB.

How? Must it be fed?

CASH.

Oh ay, humour is nothing, if it be not fed. Didst thou never
hear that? It's a common phrase, 'Feed my humour'.

COB.

I'll none on it: humour, avaunt, I know you not, begone. Let
who will make hungry meals for your monstership, it shall not
be I. Feed you, quoth he? 'Slid, I ha' much ado, to feed myself;
especially, on these lean rascally days, too; and't had been any
other day, but a fasting day – a plague on them all for me – by
this light, one might have done [56][the commonwealth] good
service, and have drowned them all i' the flood, two or three
hundred thousand years ago. Oh, I do stomach them hugely! I
have a maw now, and 'twere for Sir Bevis his horse, against
'hem.

CASH.

I pray thee, good Cob, what makes thee so out of love with
fasting days?

COB.

Marry that, which will make any man out of love with 'hem, I
think: their bad conditions, and you will needs know. First,
they are of a Flemish breed, I am sure on't, for they ravin up
more butter, than all the days of the week, beside; next, they
stink of fish, and leek-porridge miserably: thirdly, they'll keep
a man devoutly hungry, all day, and at night send him supper-
less to bed.

[56] God

CASH.

Indeed, these are faults, Cob.

COB.

Nay, and this were all, 'twere something, but they are the only known enemies, to my generation. A fasting day, no sooner comes, but my lineage goes to rack, poor cobs they smoke for it, they are made martyrs o' the gridiron, they melt in passion: and your maids too know this, and yet would have me turn Hannibal, and eat my own fish, and blood: my princely coz (*He pulls out a red herring*), fear nothing; I have not the heart to devour you, and I might be made as rich as King Cophetua. Oh, that I had room for my tears, I could weep salt water enough, now, to preserve the lives of ten thousand of my kin. But I may curse none but these filthy Almanacs, for an'twere not for them, these days of persecution would ne'er be known. I'll be hanged, an' some fishmonger's son do not make of 'hem; and puts in more fasting days than he should do, because he would utter his father's dried stock-fish, and stinking conger.

CASH.

'Slight, peace, thou'lt be beaten like a stock-fish, else: here is Master Matthew. Now must I look out for a messenger to my master.

{*Exit with Cob.*}

{*Enter*} Wellbred, Ed. Kno'well, Brainworm, Bobadill, Matthew {*and*} Stephen.

WELLBRED.

Beshrew me, but it was an absolute good jest, and exceedingly well carried!

ED. KNO'WELL.

Ay, and our ignorance maintained it as well, did it not?

WELLBRED.

Yes faith, but was't possible thou should'st not know him? I forgive Master Stephen, for he is stupidity itself!

ED. KNO'WELL.

'Fore God, not I, [and I might have been joined patten with one of the seven wise masters, for knowing him.] He had so writhen himself, into [the habit of] one of your [poor infantry, your] decayed, ruinous, worm-eaten gentlemen of the round: [such as have vowed to sit on the skirts of the city, let your provost, and his half-dozen of halbadiers do what they can; and have translated begging out of the old hackney pace, to a fine easy amble, and made it run as smooth, off the tongue, as a shove-groat shilling. Into the likeness of one of these reformados had he moulded himself so perfectly, observing every trick of their action, as varying the accent, swearing with an emphasis, indeed all, with so special, and exquisite a grace,] that – hadst thou seen him – thou wouldst have sworn, he might have been [sergeant-major, if not] lieutenant-colonel to the regiment.

WELLBRED.

Why, Brainworm, who would have thought thou hadst been such an artificer?

ED. KNO'WELL.

An artificer! An architect! [Except a man had studied begging all his lifetime, and been a weaver of language, from his infancy, for the clothing of it!] I never saw his rival.

[WELLBRED.

Where got'st thou this coat, I marle?

BRAINWORM.

Of a Houndsditch man, sir. One of the devil's near kinsmen, a broker.

WELLBRED.

That cannot be, if the proverb hold; for, a crafty knave needs no broker.

BRAINWORM.

True sir, but I did need a broker, ergo.

WELLBRED.

Well put off – no crafty knave, you'll say.

ED. KNO'WELL.

Tut, he has more of these shifts.

BRAINWORM.

And yet where I have one, the broker has ten, sir.]

{*Enter*} Cash.

CASH.

Francis, Martin, ne'er a one to be found, now? What a spite's this?

WELLBRED.

How now, Thomas? Is my brother Kitely, within?

CASH.

No sir, my master went forth e'en now: but Master Downright is within. Cob, what Cob! Is he gone too?

WELLBRED.

Whither went your master? Thomas, canst thou tell?

CASH.

I know not, to Justice Clement's I think, sir. [Cob!

{*Exit Cash.*}

ED. KNO'WELL.

Justice Clement, what's he?

WELLBRED.

Why, dost thou not know him? He is a city magistrate, a justice
here, an excellent good lawyer, and a great scholar: but the only
mad, merry, old fellow in Europe! I showed him you, the other
day.

ED. KNO'WELL.

Oh, is that he? I remember him now. Good faith, and he has a
very strange presence, methinks; it shows as if he stood out of
the rank, from other men: I have heard many of his jests i' the
university. They say, he will commit a man, for taking the wall,
of his horse.

WELLBRED.

Ay, or wearing his cloak of one shoulder, or serving of God:
anything indeed, if it come in the way of his humour.

Cash goes in and out calling.

CASH.]

Gasper, Martin, Cob! 'Heart, where should they be, trow?

BOBADILL.

Master Kitely's man, 'pray thee vouchsafe us the lighting of
this match.

CASH.

Fire on your match, no time but now to vouchsafe? Francis,
Cob!

BOBADILL.

Body of me! Here's the remainder of seven pound, since yesterday was seven-night. 'Tis your right Trinidado! Did you never
take any, Master Stephen?

STEPHEN.

No truly, sir: but I'll learn to take it now, since you commend
it, so.

BOBADILL.

Sir, believe me, upon my relation, for what I tell you, the world
shall not reprove. I have been in the Indies, where this herb
grows, where neither myself, nor a dozen gentlemen before, of
my knowledge, have received the taste of any other nutriment,
in the world, for the space of one and twenty weeks, but the
fume of this simple only. Therefore, it cannot be, but 'tis most
divine! Further, take it in the nature, in the true kind so, it
makes an antidote, that, had you taken the most deadly poison-
ous plant in all Italy, it should expel it, and clarify you, with as
much ease, as I speak. And, for your green wound, your

Balsamum, and your St. John's wort are all mere gulleries, and
trash to it, especially your Trinidado: your Nicotian is good too.
I could say what I know of the virtue of it, for the expulsion of
rheums, raw humours, crudities, obstructions, with a thousand
of this kind; but I profess myself no quacksalver. Only, thus
much, by Hercules, I do hold it, and will affirm it, before any
prince in Europe, to be the most sovereign, and precious weed,
that ever the earth tendered to the use of man.

ED. KNO'WELL.

This speech would ha' done decently in a tobacco-trader's
mouth!

{Enter Cash with Cob.}

CASH.

At Justice Clement's, he is: in the middle of Coleman Street.

COB.

Oh, oh!

BOBADILL.

Where's the match I gave thee? Master Kitely's man?

CASH.

Would his match, and he, and pipe, and all were at Santo
Domingo! I had forgot it.

{Exit.}

COB.

By God's me, I marle, what pleasure, or felicity they have in
taking this roguish tobacco! It's good for nothing, but to choke
a man, and fill him full of smoke, and embers: there were four
died out of one house, last week, with taking of it, and two more
the bell went for, yesternight; one of them, they say, will ne'er
scape it: he voided a bushel of soot yesterday, upward, and
downward. By the stocks, an' there were no wiser men than I,
I'd have it present whipping, man, or woman, that should but
deal with a tobacco-pipe; why, it will stifle them all in the end,
as many as use it; it's little better than ratsbane [, or rosaker].

Bobadill beats {Cob} with a cudgel.

ALL.

Oh, good Captain, hold, hold.

BOBADILL.

You base cullion, you.

{Enter Cash.}

CASH.

Sir, here's your match: come, thou must needs be talking, too, thou'rt well enough served.

COB.

Nay, he will not meddle with his match, I warrant you: well it shall be a dear beating, and I live.

BOBADILL.

Do you prate? Do you murmur?

ED. KNO'WELL.

Nay, good Captain, will you regard the humour of a fool? Away, knave.

WELLBRED.

Thomas, get him away.

{*Exit Cash with Cob.*}

BOBADILL.

A whoreson filthy slave, a dung-worm,[57] an excrement! Body o' Caesar, but that I scorn to let forth so mean a spirit, I'd ha' stabbed him, to the earth.

WELLBRED.

Marry, [58][the law] forbid, sir.

BOBADILL.

By Pharaoh's foot, I would have done it.

STEPHEN.

{*Aside*} Oh, he swears admirably! By Pharaoh's foot! Body o' Caesar! I shall never do it, sure, upon [59][mine honour], and by St. George, no, I ha' not the right grace.

MATTHEW.

Master Stephen, will you any? By this air, the most divine tobacco, that ever I drunk!

STEPHEN.

None, I thank you, sir. Oh, this gentleman does it, rarely too! But nothing like the other. (*Master Stephen is practising, to the post.*) By this air, as I am a gentleman: by –

BRAINWORM.

{*Pointing at Stephen.*} Master, glance, glance! Master Wellbred!

{*Exeunt Bobadill and Matthew.*}

STEPHEN.

As I have somewhat to be saved, I protest –

WELLBRED.

You are a fool: it needs no affidavit.

ED. KNO'WELL.

Cousin, will you any tobacco?

STEPHEN.

I sir! Upon my [60][reputation –]

ED. KNO'WELL.

How now, cousin!

STEPHEN.

I protest, as I am a gentleman, but no soldier, indeed –

WELLBRED.

No, Master Stephen! As I remember your name is entered in the Artillery Garden?

STEPHEN.

Ay sir, that's true: cousin, may I swear, as I am a soldier, by that?

ED. KNO'WELL.

Oh yes, that you may. It's all you have for your money.

STEPHEN.

Then, as I am a gentleman, and a soldier, it is divine tobacco!

WELLBRED.

But soft, where's Master Matthew? Gone?

BRAINWORM.

No, sir, they went in here.

WELLBRED.

Oh, let's follow them: Master Matthew is gone to salute his mistress, in verse. We shall ha' the happiness, to hear some of his poetry, now. He never comes unfurnished. Brainworm?

STEPHEN.

Brainworm? Where? Is this Brainworm?

ED. KNO'WELL.

Ay, cousin, no words of it, upon your gentility.

STEPHEN.

Not I, body of me, by this air, St. George, and the foot of Pharaoh.

WELLBRED.

Rare! Your cousin's discourse is simply drawn out with oaths.

---

[57] *Insert:* a turd,
[58] God
[59] my salvation
[60] salvation –

ED. KNO'WELL.

'Tis larded with 'hem. A kind of French dressing, if you love it.

{*Exeunt.*}

Scene iii

{*Coleman Street. A Room in Justice Clement's House. Enter*} *Kitely* {*and*} *Cob.*

KITELY.

Ha? How many are there, sayest thou?

COB.

Marry sir, your brother, Master Wellbred.

KITELY.

Tut, beside him: what strangers are there, man?

COB.

Strangers? Let me see, one, two; mass I know not well, there are so many.

KITELY.

How? So many?

COB.

Ay, there's some five, or six of them, at the most.

KITELY.

{*Aside*} A swarm, a swarm,
Spite of the devil, how they sting my head
With forked stings, thus wide, and large! – But, Cob,
How long hast thou been coming hither, Cob?

COB.

A little while, sir.

KITELY.   Didst thou come running?

COB.   No, sir.

KITELY.

{*Aside.*} Nay, then I am familiar with thy haste!
Bane to my fortunes: what meant I to marry?
I, that before was ranked in such content,
My mind at rest too, in so soft a peace,
Being free master of mine own free thoughts,
And now become a slave? What? Never sigh,
Be of good cheer, man: for thou art a cuckold,
'Tis done, 'tis done! Nay, when such flowing store,
Plenty itself, falls in my wife's lap,

The cornucopiae will be mine, I know. – But, Cob,
What entertainment had they? I am sure
My sister, and my wife, would bid them welcome! Ha?

COB.

Like enough, sir, yet, I heard not a word of it.

KITELY.

No: their lips were sealed with kisses, and the voice
Drowned in a flood of joy, at their arrival,
Had lost her motion, state, and faculty.
Cob, which of them was't, that first kissed my wife?
My sister, I should say. My wife, alas,
I fear not her: ha? Who was it, say'st thou?

COB.

By my troth, sir, will you have the truth of it?

KITELY.

Oh ay, good Cob: I pray thee, heartily.

COB.

Then, I am a vagabond, and fitter for Bridewell, than your worship's company, if I saw anybody to be kissed, unless they would have kissed the post, in the middle of the warehouse; for there I left them all, at their tobacco, with a pox.

KITELY.

How? Were they not gone in, then, ere thou cam'st?

COB.

Oh no sir.

KITELY.

Spite of the devil! What do I stay here, then? Cob, follow me.

{*Exit.*}

COB.

Nay, soft and fair, I have eggs on the spit; I cannot go yet, sir. Now am I for some five and fifty reasons hammering, hammering revenge: oh, for three or four gallons of vinegar, to sharpen my wits. Revenge: vinegar revenge: vinegar, and mustard revenge: nay, and he had not lien in my house, 'twould never have grieved me, but being my guest, one, that I'll be sworn, my wife has lent him her smock off her back, while his one shirt has been at washing; pawned her neckerchers for clean bands for him; sold almost all my platters, to buy him tobacco; and he to turn monster of ingratitude, and strike his lawful host! Well, I hope to raise up an host of fury for't: here comes Justice Clement.

{*Enter*} *Clement, Kno'well and Formal.*

CLEMENT.
What's Master Kitely gone? Roger?

FORMAL.
Ay, sir.

CLEMENT.
'Heart o' me! What made him leave us so abruptly? – How now, sirrah? What make you here? What would you have, ha?

COB.
And't please your worship, I am a poor neighbour of your worship's –

CLEMENT.
A poor neighbour of mine? Why, speak poor neighbour.

COB.
I dwell, sir, at the sign of the Water-tankard, hard by the Green Lattice: I have paid scot, and lot there, any time this eighteen years.

CLEMENT.
To the Green Lattice?

COB.
No, sir, to the parish: marry, I have seldom scaped scot-free, at the Lattice.

CLEMENT.
Oh, well! What business has my poor neighbour with me?

COB.
And't like your worship, I am come, to crave the peace of your worship.

CLEMENT.
Of me knave? Peace of me, knave? Did I e'er hurt thee? Or threaten thee? Or wrong thee? Ha?

COB.
No, sir, but your worship's warrant, for one that has wronged me, sir: his arms are at too much liberty, I would fain have them bound to a treaty of peace, an' my credit could compass it, with your worship.

CLEMENT.
Thou goest far enough about for't, I'm sure.

KNO'WELL.
Why, dost thou go in danger of thy life for him? Friend?

COB.
No sir; but I go in danger of my death, every hour, by his means: an I die, within a twelve-month and a day, I may swear, by the law of the land, that he killed me.

CLEMENT.
How? How knave? Swear he killed thee? And by the law? What pretence? What colour hast thou for that?

COB.
Mary, and't please your worship, both black, and blue; colour enough, I warrant you. I have it here, to show your worship.

{*He shows his bruises.*}

CLEMENT.
What is he, that gave you this, sirrah?

COB.
A gentleman, and a soldier, he says he is, o' the city here.

CLEMENT.
A soldier o' the city? What call you him?

COB.
Captain Bobadill.

CLEMENT.
Bobadill? And why did he bob, and beat you, sirrah? How began the quarrel betwixt you: ha? Speak truly knave, I advise you.

COB.
Marry, indeed, and please your worship, only because I spake against their vagrant tobacco, as I came by 'hem, when they were taking on't, for nothing else.

CLEMENT.
Ha? You speak against tobacco? Formal, his name.

FORMAL.
What's your name, sirrah?

COB.
Oliver, sir. Oliver Cob, sir.

CLEMENT.
Tell Oliver Cob, he shall go to the jail, Formal.

FORMAL.
Oliver Cob, my master, Justice Clement, says, you shall go to the jail.

COB.
Oh, I beseech your worship, for God's sake, dear Master Justice.

CLEMENT.
Nay, God's precious: and such drunkards, and tankards, as you

are, come to dispute of tobacco once; I have done! Away with
him.

COB.

Oh, good Master Justice, sweet old gentleman.

KNO'WELL.

Sweet Oliver, would I could do thee any good: Justice Clement,
let me entreat you, sir.

CLEMENT.

What? A threadbare rascal! A beggar! A slave that never drunk
out of better than pisspot metal in his life! And he to deprave,
and abuse the virtue of an herb, so generally received in the
courts of princes, the chambers of nobles, the bowers of sweet
ladies, the cabins of soldiers! Roger, away with him, by God's
[61][precious] – I say, go to.

COB.

Dear Master Justice; let me be beaten again, I have deserved it:
but not the prison, I beseech you.

KNO'WELL.

Alas, poor Oliver!

CLEMENT.

Roger, make him a warrant. He shall not go: I but fear the
knave.

FORMAL.

Do not stink, sweet Oliver, you shall not go, my master will give
you a warrant.

COB.

Oh, the Lord maintain his worship, his worthy worship.

CLEMENT.

Away, dispatch him.

{Exeunt Formal and Cob.}

How now, Master Kno'well! [62][In dumps? In dumps! Come,
this becomes not.]

KNO'WELL.

Sir, would I could not feel my cares –

CLEMENT.

Your cares are nothing! They are like my cap, soon put on, and
as soon put off. What? Your son is old enough, to govern
himself: let him run his course, it's the only way to make him a
staid man. If he were an unthrift, a ruffian, a drunkard, or a
licentious liver, then you had reason; you had reason to take
care: but, being none of these, [63][mirth's my witness,] an' I had

twice so many cares, as you have, I'd drown them all in a cup of
sack. Come, come, let's try it: I muse, your parcel of a soldier
returns not all this while.

{Exeunt.}

---

[61] passion
[62] God's pity, man, be merry, be merry,
leave these dumps.
[63] God's passion

ACT IV

Scene i

{A Room in Kitely's House. Enter} Downright {and} Dame Kitely.

DOWNRIGHT.
Well sister, I tell you true: and you'll find it so, in the end.

DAME KITELY.
Alas brother, what would you have me to do? I cannot help it: you see, my brother brings 'hem in, here, they are his friends.

DOWNRIGHT.
His friends. His fiends. [64][Slud,] they do nothing but haunt him, up and down, like a sort of unlucky sprites, and tempt him to all manner of villainy, that can be thought of. Well, by this light, a little thing would make me play the devil with some of 'em; and 'twere not more for your husband's sake, than anything else, I'd make the house too hot for the best on 'hem: they should [say, and] swear, hell were broken loose, ere they went hence. But, by God's [65][will], 'tis nobody's fault, but yours: for, an' you had done, as you might have done, they should have been parboiled, and baked too, every mother's son, ere they should ha' come in, e'er one of 'hem.

DAME KITELY.
God's my life! Did you ever hear the like? What a strange man is this! Could I keep out all them, think you? I should put myself, against half a dozen men? Should I? Good faith, you'd mad the patient'st body in the world, to hear you talk so, without any sense, or reason!

{Enter} Mistress Bridget, Master Matthew, {and} Bobadill; {followed, at a little distance, by} Wellbred, Stephen, Ed. Kno'well {and} Brainworm.

BRIDGET.
Servant, in troth, you are too prodigal
Of your wit's treasure, thus to pour it forth,
Upon so mean a subject, as my worth?

MATTHEW.
You say well, mistress; and I mean, as well.

DOWNRIGHT.
Hoy-day, here is stuff!

[66][WELLBRED.
Oh, now stand close: pray heaven, she can get him to read: he should do it, of his own natural impudency.]

BRIDGET.
Servant, what is this same, I pray you?

MATTHEW.
Marry, an elegy, an elegy, an odd toy –

DOWNRIGHT.
To mock an ape withal. Oh, I could sew up his mouth, now.

DAME KITELY.
Sister, I pray you let's hear it.

DOWNRIGHT.
Are you rhyme-given, too?

MATTHEW.
Mistress, I'll read it, if you please.

BRIDGET.
Pray you do, servant.

DOWNRIGHT.
Oh, here's no foppery! Death, I can endure the stocks, better.

{Exit.}

ED. KNO'WELL.
What ails thy brother? Can he not hold his water, at reading of a ballad.

WELLBRED.
Oh, no: a rhyme to him, is worse than cheese, or a bagpipe. But, mark, you lose the protestation.

MATTHEW.
Faith, I did it in a humour; I know not how it is: but, please you come near, sir. This gentleman has judgement, he knows how to censure of a – pray you sir, you can judge.

STPEHEN.
Not I, sir: [67][upon my reputation,] and, by the foot of Pharaoh.

WELLBRED.
Oh, chide your cousin, for swearing.

ED. KNO'WELL.
Not I, so long as he does not forswear himself.

---

[64] 'Sblood
[65] bread
[66] ED. KNO'WELL.
Oh, now stand close: pray heaven, she can get him to read.
WELLBRED.
He should do it, of his own natural impudency.
[67] as I have a soul to be saved,

BOBADILL.

Master Matthew, you abuse the expectation of your dear mistress, and her fair sister: fie, while you live, avoid this prolixity.

MATTHEW.

I shall, sir: well, *incipere dulce*.

ED. KNO'WELL.

How! *Insipere dulce*? A sweet thing to be a fool, indeed.

[WELLBRED.

What, do you take *incipere*, in that sense?

ED. KNO'WELL.

You do not? You? This was your villainy, to gull him with a *mot*.

WELLBRED.

Oh, the benchers' phrase: *pauca verba, pauca verba.*]

MATTHEW.

Rare creature, let me speak without offence,
Would God my rude words had the influence,
To rule thy thoughts, as thy fair looks do mine,
Then should'st thou be his prisoner, who is thine.

ED. KNO'WELL.

This is in *Hero and Leander*.

WELLBRED.

Oh, ay! Peace, we shall have more of this.

MATTHEW.

Be not unkind, and fair, misshapen stuff
Is of behaviour boisterous, and rough.

WELLBRED.

How you like that, sir?

Master Stephen answers with shaking his head.

ED. KNO'WELL.

[68]['Slight], he shakes his head like a bottle, to feel and there be any brain in it!

MATTHEW.

But observe the catastrophe, now,
And I in duty will exceed all other,
As you in beauty do excel love's mother.

ED. KNO'WELL.

[Well, I'll have him free of the wit-brokers, for] he utters nothing, but stol'n remnants.

WELLBRED.

Oh, forgive it him.

ED. KNO'WELL.

A filching rogue? [69][Hang him. And,] from the dead? It's worse than sacrilege.

{*Wellbred, Ed. Kno'well and Stephen come forward.*}

WELLBRED.

Sister, what ha' you here? Verses? Pray you, let's see. Who made these verses? They are excellent good!

MATTHEW.

Oh, Master Wellbred, 'tis your disposition to say so sir. They were good i' the morning, I made 'hem, extempore, this morning.

WELLBRED.

How? Extempore?

MATTHEW.

I would I might be [70][hanged] else; ask Captain Bobadill. He saw me write them, at the – pox on it! – the [71][Star], yonder.

[BRAINWORM.

Can he find, in his heart, to curse the stars, so?

ED. KNO'WELL

Faith, his are even with him: they ha' cursed him enough already.]

STEPHEN.

Cousin, how do you like this gentleman's verses?

ED. KNO'WELL.

Oh, admirable! The best that ever I heard, coz!

STEPHEN.

Body o' Caesar! They are admirable! The best, that ever I heard, as I am a soldier.

{*Enter Downright.*}

DOWNRIGHT.

I am vexed, I can hold ne'er a bone of me still! [72][Heart!] I think, they mean to build, and breed here!

WELLBRED.

Sister, you have a simple servant, here, that crowns your beauty, with such encomiums, and devices: you may see, what

---

[68] 'Sblood
[69] A pox on him. Hang him. Steal
[70] damn'd
[71] Mitre
[72] 'Sblood

it is to be the mistress of a wit that can make your perfections so transparent, that every blear eye may look through them, and see him drowned over head, and ears, in the deep well of desire. Sister Kitely, I marvel, you get you not a servant, that can rhyme, and do tricks, too.

DOWNRIGHT.
Oh monster! Impudence itself! Tricks?

DAME KITELY.
Tricks, brother? What tricks?

BRIDGET.
Nay, speak, I pray you, what tricks?

DAME KITELY.
Ay, never spare any body here; but say, what tricks?

BRIDGET.
Passion of my heart! Do tricks?

WELLBRED.
'Slight, here's a trick vied, and revied! Why, you monkeys, you? What a caterwauling do you keep? Has he not given you rhymes, and verses, and tricks?

DOWNRIGHT.
Oh, the fiend!

WELLBRED.
Nay, you – lamp of virginity, that take it in snuff so! Come, and cherish this tame 'poetical fury', in your servant, [you'll be begged else, shortly, for a concealment: go to,] reward his muse. You cannot give him less than a shilling, in conscience, for the book, he had it out of, cost him a [73][teston], at least. How now, gallants? Master Matthew? Captain? What? All sons of silence? No spirit?

DOWNRIGHT.
Come, you might practise your ruffian-tricks somewhere else, [and not here,] I wuss; this is no tavern, [nor drinking-school,] to vent your exploits in.

WELLBRED.
How now! Whose cow has calved?

DOWNRIGHT.
Marry, that has mine, sir. Nay, boy, never look askance at me, for the matter; I'll tell you of it, [74][I, sir,] you, and your companions, mend yourselves, when I ha' done.

WELLBRED.
My companions?

DOWNRIGHT.
Yes sir, your companions, so I say,[75] I am not afraid of you, nor them neither: your hang-byes here. You must have your poets, and your potlings, your soldados, and foolados, [to follow you up and down the city,] and here they must come to domineer, and swagger. Sirrah, you, ballad-singer, and slops, your fellow there, get you out; get you home: or, by this steel, I'll cut off your ears, and that, presently.

WELLBRED.
'Slight, stay, let's see what he dare do: cut off his ears? Cut a whetstone. You are an ass, do you see? Touch any man here, and by this hand, I'll run my rapier to the hilts in you.

DOWNRIGHT.
Yea, that would I fain see, boy.

They all draw, and they of the house make out to part them.

DAME KITELY.
Oh Jesu! Murder. Thomas, Gaspar!

BRIDGET.
Help, help, Thomas.

{Enter} Cash {and Servants.}

ED. KNO'WELL.
Gentlemen, forebear, I pray you.

BOBADILL.
Well, sirrah, you, Holofernes: by my hand, I will pink your flesh, full of holes, with my rapier for this; I will, by this good heaven (*They offer to fight again, and are parted*): nay, let him come, let him come, gentlemen, by the body of St. George, I'll not kill him.

CASH.
Hold, hold, good gentlemen.

DOWNRIGHT.
You whoreson, bragging coystril.

{Enter} Kitely.

KITELY.
Why, how now? What's the matter? What's the stir here?
Whence springs this quarrel? Thomas! Where is he?
Put up your weapons, and put off this rage.
My wife and sister, they are the cause of this,

---

[73] sixpence
[74] by God's bread, ay, sir, and
[75] *Insert:* 'Sblood

What, Thomas? Where is this knave?

CASH.   Here, sir.

WELLBRED.
Come, let's go: this is one of my brother's ancient humours, this.

STEPHEN.
I am glad, nobody was hurt by his ancient humour.

{Exeunt Wellbred, Stephen, Ed. Kno'well, Matthew, Bobadill
and Brainworm.}

KITELY.
Why, how now, brother, who enforced this brawl?

DOWNRIGHT.
A sort of lewd rakehells, that care neither for God, nor the devil! And, they must come here to read ballads, and roguery, and trash! I'll mar the knot of 'hem ere I sleep, perhaps: especially Bob, there: he that's all manner of shapes! And 'Songs, and sonnets', his fellow.

BRIDGET.
Brother, indeed, you are too violent,
Too sudden, in your humour: and, you know
My brother Wellbred's temper will not bear
Any reproof, chiefly in such a presence,
Where every slight disgrace, he should receive,
Might wound him in opinion, and respect.

DOWNRIGHT.
Respect? What talk you of respect 'mong such,
As ha' nor spark of manhood, nor good manners?
'Sdeins I am ashamed, to hear you! Respect?

{Exit.}

BRIDGET.
Yes, there was one a civil gentleman,
And very worthily demeaned himself!

KITELY.
Oh, that was some love of yours, sister!

BRIDGET.
A love of mine? I would it were no worse, brother!
You'd pay my portion sooner, than you think for.

DAME KITELY.
Indeed, he seemed to be a gentleman of an exceeding fair disposition, and of very excellent good parts!

{Exeunt Dame Kitely and Bridget.}

KITELY.
{Aside} Her love, by heaven! My wife's minion!
Fair disposition? Excellent good parts?
Death, these phrases are intolerable!
Good parts? How should she know his parts?
His parts? Well, well, well, well, well, well!
It is too plain, too clear. – Thomas, come hither.
What, are they gone?

CASH.   Ay, sir, they went in.
My mistress, and your sister –

KITELY.
Are any of the gallants within?

CASH.
No, sir, they are all gone.

KITELY.
Art thou sure of it?

CASH.
I can assure you, sir.

KITELY.
What gentleman was that they praised so, Thomas?

CASH.
One, they call him Master Kno'well, a handsome young gentleman, sir.

KITELY.
{Aside} Ay, I thought so: my mind gave me as much.
I'll die, but they have hid him i' the house,
Somewhere; I'll go and search. – Go with me, Thomas.
Be true to me, and thou shalt find me a master.

{Exeunt.}

Scene ii

{The Lane before Cob's House. Enter} Cob.

COB.
{Knocking} What Tib, Tib, I say!

TIB.
{From within} How now, what cuckold is that knocks so hard?
{She opens the door} Oh, husband, is't you? What's the news?

COB.

Nay, you have stunned me, i' faith! You ha' gi'en me a knock o'
the forehead, will stick by me! Cuckold? 'Slid, cuckold?

TIB.

Away, you fool, did I know it was you, that knocked? Come,
come, you may call me as bad, when you list.

COB.

May I? Tib, you are a whore.

TIB.

You lie in your throat, husband.

COB.

How, the lie? And in my throat too? Do you long to be stabbed,
ha?

TIB.

Why, you are no soldier, I hope?

COB.

Oh, must you be stabbed by a soldier? Mass, that's true! When
was Bobadill here? Your captain? That rogue, that foist, that
fencing Burgullian? I'll tickle him, i' faith.

TIB.

Why, what's the matter? Trow!

COB.

Oh, he has basted me, rarely, sumptuously! But I have it here in
black and white; {*Pulls out his warrant.*} for his black, and blue:
shall [76][pay] him. Oh, the Justice! The honestest old brave
Trojan in London! I do honour the very flea of his dog. A
plague on him though, he put me once in a villainous filthy fear;
marry, it vanished away, like the smoke of tobacco; but I was
smoked soundly first. I thank the devil, and his good angel, my
guest. Well, wife, or Tib – which you will – get you in, and lock
the door, I charge you, let nobody in to you; wife, no body in, to
you: those are my words. Not Captain Bob himself, nor the
fiend, in his likeness; you are a woman; you have flesh and
blood enough in you, to be tempted: therefore, keep the door,
shut, upon all comers.

TIB.

I warrant you, there shall nobody enter here, without my
consent.

COB.

Nor with your consent, sweet Tib, and so I leave you.

TIB.

It's more, than you know, whether you leave me so.

COB.

How?

TIB.

Why, sweet.

COB.

Tut, sweet, or sour, thou art a flower,
Keep close thy door, I ask no more.

{*Exeunt.*}

Scene iii

{*A Room in the Windmill Tavern. Enter*} Ed. Kno'well, Wellbred,
Stephen {*and*} Brainworm {*disguised as before*}.

ED. KNO'WELL.

Well Brainworm, perform this business, happily, and thou
makest a purchase of my love, forever.

WELLBRED.

[77][I' faith, now let thy spirits use their best faculties. But, at any
hand, remember the message, to my brother:] for, there's no
other means, to start him.

BRAINWORM.

I warrant you, sir, fear nothing: I have a nimble soul has waked
all [78][forces of my phant'sie,] by this time, and put 'hem in true
motion. What you have possessed me withal, I'll discharge it
amply, sir. Make [it] no question.

WELLBRED.

Forth, and prosper, Brainworm.

{*Exit Brainworm.*}

Faith, Ned, how dost thou approve of my abilities in this
device?

ED. KNO'WELL.

Troth, well, howsoever: but, it will come excellent, if it take.

WELLBRED.

Take, man? Why, it cannot choose but take, if the circumstances miscarry not: but, tell me, ingenuously, dost thou affect
my sister Bridget, as thou pretend'st?

[76] sauce

[77] I'faith, now let thy spirits put on their best habit. But, at any hand,
remember the message, to my brother Kitely,

[78] my imaginative forces

ED. KNO'WELL.

Friend, am I worth belief?

WELLBRED.

Come, do not protest. In faith, she is a maid of good ornament, and much modesty: and, except I conceived very worthily of her, thou shouldest not have her.

ED. KNO'WELL.

Nay, that I am afraid will be a question yet, whether I shall have her, or no?

WELLBRED.

'Slid, thou shalt have her; by this light, thou shalt.

ED. KNO'WELL.

Nay, do not swear.

WELLBRED.

By [79][this hand], thou shalt have her: I'll go fetch her, presently. Point, but where to meet, and as I am an honest man, I'll bring her.

ED. KNO'WELL.

Hold, hold, be temperate.

WELLBRED.

Why, by – what shall I swear by? Thou shalt have her, [80][as I am –]

ED. KNO'WELL.

'Pray thee, be at peace, I am satisfied: and do believe, thou wilt omit no offered occasion, to make my desires complete.

WELLBRED.

Thou shalt see, and know, I will not.

Scene iv

{*The Old Jewry. Enter*} *Formal* {*and*} *Kno'well.*

FORMAL.

Was your man a soldier, sir?

KNO'WELL.

Ay, a knave, I took him begging o' the way,
This morning, as I came over Moorfields!
Oh, here he is! Yo' have made fair speed, believe me:
Where, i' the name of sloth, could you be thus –

{*Enter Brainworm, disguised as before.*}

BRAINWORM.

Marry, [81][peace be] my comfort, where I thought I should have had so little comfort of your worship's service.

KNO'WELL.

How so?

BRAINWORM.

Oh, sir! Your coming to the city, your entertainment of me, and your sending me to watch – indeed, all the circumstances either of your charge, or my employment, are as open to your son, as to yourself!

KNO'WELL.

How should that be! Unless that villain, Brainworm,
Have told him of the letter, and discovered
All that I strictly charged him to conceal? 'Tis so!

BRAINWORM.

I am, partly, o' the faith, 'tis so indeed.

KNO'WELL.

But, how should he know thee to be my man?

BRAINWORM.

Nay, sir, I cannot tell; unless it be by the black art! Is not your son a scholar, sir?

KNO'WELL.

Yes, but I hope his soul is not allied
Unto such hellish practices: if it were,
I had just cause to weep my part in him,
And curse the time of his creation.
But, where didst thou find them, Fitzsword?

BRAINWORM.

You should rather ask, where they found me, sir, for, I'll be sworn I was going along in the street, thinking nothing, when, of a sudden, a voice calls, 'Master Kno'well's man!'; another cries, 'Soldier!': and thus, half a dozen of 'hem, till they had called me within a house where I no sooner came, but they seemed men, and out flew all their rapiers at my bosom, with some three or fourscore oaths to accompany 'hem, and all to tell me, I was but a dead man, if I did not confess where you were, and how I was employed, and about what; which, when they could not get out of me – [82][as I protest,] they must ha' dissected, and made an anatomy o'me, first, and so I told 'hem –

[79] St Mark,
[80] by my soul
[81] God's
[82] God's my judge,

they locked me up into a room i' the top of a high house, whence, by great miracle, having a light heart, I slid down, by a bottom of packthread, into the street, and so scaped. But, sir, thus much I can assure you, for I heard it, while I was locked up, there were a great many rich merchants, and brave citizens' wives with 'hem at a feast, and your son, Master Edward, withdrew with one of 'hem, and has pointed to meet her anon, at one Cob's house, a water-bearer, that dwells by the wall. Now, there, your worship shall be sure to take him, for there he preys, and fail he will not.

KNO'WELL.

Nor, will I fail, to break his match, I doubt not. [83][Go thou, along] with Justice Clement's man, [And stay there for me.] At one Cob's house, say'st thou?

BRAINWORM.

Ay sir, there you shall have him.

{*Exit Kno'well.*}

Yes? Invisible? Much wench, or much son? 'Slight, when he has stayed there, three or four hours, travailing with the expectation of wonders, and at length be delivered of air: Oh, the sport, that I should then take, to look on him, if I durst! But, now, I mean to appear no more afore him in this shape. I have another trick, to act, yet. [Oh, that I were so happy; as to light on a nupson, now, of this Justice's novice. – Sir, I make you stay somewhat long.][84]

FORMAL.

[Not a whit, sir.][85] 'Pray you, what do you mean? Sir?

BRAINWORM.

I was putting up some papers –

FORMAL.

You ha' been lately in the wars, sir, it seems.

BRAINWORM.

Marry have I, sir; to my loss: and expense of all, almost –

FORMAL.

Troth sir, I would be glad to bestow a pottle of wine o'you, if it please you to accept it –

BRAINWORM.

Oh, sir –

FORMAL.

But, to hear the manner of your services, and your devices in the wars, they say they be very strange, and not like those a man reads in the Roman histories, or sees, at Mile End.

BRAINWORM.

[86][No, I assure you,] sir, why, at any time when it please you, I shall be ready to discourse to you, all I know: {*Aside*} and more too, somewhat.

FORMAL.

No better time, than now, sir; well go to the [87][Windmill]: there we shall have a cup of neat grist, we call it. I pray you, sir, let me request you, to the [88][Windmill].

BRAINWORM.

I'll follow you, sir, {*Aside*} and make grist o'you, if I have good luck.

Scene v

{*Moorfields. Enter*} Matthew, Ed. Kno'well, Bobadill {*and*} Stephen.

MATTHEW.

Sir, did your eyes ever taste the like clown of him, where we were today, Master Wellbred's half-brother? I think, the whole earth cannot show his parallel, by [89][this daylight.]

ED. KNO'WELL.

We were now speaking of him: Captain Bobadill tells me, he is fall'n foul o' you, too.

MATTHEW.

Oh, ay, sir, he threatened me, with the bastinado.

BOBADILL.

Ay, but I think, I taught you prevention, this morning, for that – You shall kill him, beyond question: if you be so generously minded.

MATTHEW.

Indeed, it is a most excellent trick! {*He fences.*}

BOBADILL.

Oh, you do not give spirit enough, to your motion, you are too tardy, too heavy! Oh, it must be done like lightning, hay? (*He*

---

[83] Stay thou here
[84] God save you sir.
[85] *Insert:* FORMAL.
    I thank you, good sir.
    Brainworm appears to be in pain
[86] O God, no
[87] Mermaid
[88] Mermaid
[89] Jesu

practices at a post.)

MATTHEW.

Rare Captain!

BOBADILL.

Tut, 'tis nothing, and 't be not done in a – *punto*!

ED. KNO'WELL.

Captain, did you ever prove yourself, upon any of our masters of defence, here?

MATTHEW.

Oh, good sir! Yes, I hope, he has.

BOBADILL.

I will tell you, sir. Upon my first coming to the city, after my long travail, for knowledge – in that mystery only – there came three, or four of 'hem to me, at a gentleman's house, where it was my chance to be resident, at that time, to entreat my presence at their schools, [and withal so much importuned me, that – I protest to you as I am a gentleman – I was ashamed of their rude demeanour, out of all measure:] well, I told 'hem, that to come to a public school, they should pardon me, it was opposite, in diameter, to my humour, but, if so they would give their attendance at my lodging, I protested to do them what right or favour I could, as I was a gentleman, and so forth.

ED. KNO'WELL.

So, sir, then you tried their skill?

BOBADILL.

Alas, soon tried! You shall hear sir. Within two three days after, they came; and, by [90][honesty], fair sir, believe me, I graced them exceedingly, showed them some two or three tricks of prevention, have purchased 'hem, since, a credit, to admiration! They cannot deny this: and yet now, they hate me, and why? Because I am excellent, and for no other vile reason on the earth.

ED. KNO'WELL.

This is strange, and barbarous! As ever I heard!

BOBADILL.

Nay, for a more instance of their preposterous natures, but note, sir. They have assaulted me some three, four, five, six of them together, as I have walked alone, in divers skirts i' the town, as Turnbull, Whitechapel, Shoreditch, which were then my quarters, and since upon the Exchange, at my lodging, and at my ordinary: where I have driven them afore me, the whole length of a street, in the open view of all our gallants, pitying to hurt them, believe me. Yet all this lenity will not o'ercome their spleen: they will be doing with the pismire, [91][raising a hill, a man may spurn abroad, with his foot, at pleasure. By myself], I could have slain them all, but I delight not in murder. I am loath to bear any other than this bastinado for 'hem: yet, I hold it good polity, not to go disarmed, for though I be skilful, I may be oppressed with multitudes.

ED. KNO'WELL.

Ay, [92][believe me], may you sir: and, in my conceit, our whole nation should sustain the loss by it, if it were so.

BOBADILL.

Alas, no: what's a peculiar man, to a nation? Not seen.

ED. KNO'WELL.

Oh, but your skill, sir!

BOBADILL.

Indeed, that might be some loss; but, who respects it? I will tell you, sir, by the way of private, and under seal; I am a gentleman, and live here obscure, and to myself; but, were I known to Her Majesty, and the Lords – observe me – I would undertake, upon this poor head, and life, for the public benefit of the state, not only to spare the entire lives of her subjects in general, but to save the one half, nay, three parts of her yearly charge, in holding war, and against what enemy soever. And, how would I do it, think you?

ED. KNO'WELL.

Nay, I know not, nor can I conceive.

BOBADILL.

Why thus, sir. I would select nineteen, more, to myself, throughout the land; gentlemen they should be of good spirit, strong, and able constitution, I would choose them by an instinct, a character, that I have: and I would teach these nineteen, the special rules, as your punto, your reverso, your stoccata, your imbroccata, your passada, your montanto: till they could all play very near, or altogether as well as myself. This done, say the enemy were forty thousand strong, we twenty would come into the field, the tenth of March, or thereabouts; and we would challenge twenty of the enemy; they could not, in their honour refuse [93][us], well, we would kill them: challenge twenty more, kill them; twenty more, kill them; twenty more, kill them too; and thus, would we kill, every man, his twenty a day, that's twenty score; twenty score,

---

[90] Jesu
[91] By my soul
[92] by Jesu
[93] the combat

that's two hundred; two hundred a day, five days a thousand; forty thousand; forty times five, five times forty, two hundred days kills them all up, by computation. And this, will I venture my poor gentleman-like carcass, to perform – provided there be no treason practised upon us – by fair, and discreet manhood, that is, civilly by the sword.

ED. KNO'WELL.
Why, are you so sure of your hand, Captain, at all times?

BOBADILL.
Tut, never miss thrust, upon my reputation with you.

ED. KNO'WELL.
[94]I would not stand in Downright's state, then, an' you meet him, for the wealth of any one street in London.

BOBADILL.
Why, sir, you mistake me! If he were here now, by this welkin, I would not draw my weapon on him! Let this gentleman do his mind: but, I will bastinado him, by the bright sun, wherever I meet him.

MATTHEW.
Faith, and I'll have a fling at him, at my distance.

ED. KNO'WELL.
God's so', look, where he is: yonder he goes.

Downright walks over the stage.

DOWNRIGHT.
What peevish luck have I, I cannot meet with those bragging rascals?

{*Exit.*}

BOBADILL.
It's not he? Is it?

ED. KNO'WELL.
Yes faith, it is he.

MATTHEW.
I'll be hanged, then, if that were he.

ED. KNO'WELL.
Sir, keep your hanging good, for some greater matter, for I assure you, that was he.

STEPHEN.
Upon my [95][reputation], it was he.

BOBADILL.
Had I thought it had been he, he must not have gone so: but I

can hardly be induced, to believe, it was he, yet.

ED. KNO'WELL.
That I think, sir.

{*Enter Downright.*}

But see, he is come again!

DOWNRIGHT.
Oh, Pharaoh's foot, have I found you? Come, draw, to your tools: draw, gipsy, or I'll thrash you.

BOBADILL.
Gentleman of valour, I do believe in thee, hear me –

DOWNRIGHT.
Draw your weapon, then.

BOBADILL.
Tall man, I never thought on it, till now – body of [96][me] – I had a warrant of the peace, served on me, even now, as I came along, by a water-bearer; this gentelman saw it, Master Matthew.

DOWNRIGHT.
'Sdeath, you will not draw, then?

He beats him, and disarms him: Matthew runs away.

BOBADILL.
Hold, hold, under thy favour, forbear.

DOWNRIGHT.
Prate again, as you like this, you whoreson foist, you. You'll control the point, you? Your consort is gone? Had he stayed he had shared with you, sir.

{*Exit Downright.*}

BOBADILL.
Well, gentleman, bear witness, I was bound to the peace, by this good day.

ED. KNO'WELL.
No faith, it's an ill day, Captain, never reckon it other: but, say you were bound to the peace, the law allows you, to defend yourself: that'll prove but a poor excuse.

BOBADILL.
I cannot tell, sir. I desire good construction, in fair sort. I never

---

[94] *Insert:* Mass,
[95] salvation
[96] St George

sustained the like disgrace, by heaven, sure I was struck with a planet thence, for I had no power to touch my weapon.

ED. KNO'WELL.

Ay, like enough, I have heard of many that have been beaten under a planet: go, get you to a surgeon.

{*Exit Bobadill.*}

'Slid, an' these be your tricks, your passadas, and your montantos, I'll none of them. Oh, [97][manners]! That this age should bring forth such creatures! That nature should be at leisure to make' hem! Come, coz.

STEPHEN.

Mass, I'll ha' this cloak.

ED. KNO'WELL.

God's will, 'tis Downright's.

STEPHEN.

Nay, it's mine now, another might have ta'en it up, as well as I: I'll wear it, so I will.

ED. KNO'WELL.

How, an' he see it? He'll challenge it, assure yourself.

STEPHEN.

Ay, but he shall not ha' it; I'll say, I bought it.

ED. KNO'WELL.

Take heed, you buy it not, too dear, coz.

{*Exeunt.*}

Scene vi

{*A Room in Kitely's House. Enter*} Kitely, Wellbred, Dame Kitely, {*and*} Bridget.

KITELY.

Now, trust me brother, you were much to blame,
T'incense his anger, and disturb the peace,
Of my poor house, where there are sentinels
That every minute watch, to give alarms,
Of civil war, without adjection
Of your assistance, or occasion.

WELLBRED.

No harm done, brother, I warrant you: since there is no harm done. Anger costs a man nothing: and a tall man is never his own man, till he be angry. To keep his valour in obscurity, is to keep himself, as it were, in a cloak-bag. What's a musician, unless he play? What's a tall man, unless he fight? For, indeed, all this, my wise brother stands upon, absolutely: and, that made me fall in with him, so resolutely.

DAME KITELY.

Ay, but what harm might have come of it, brother?

WELLBRED.

Might, sister? So, might the good warm clothes, your husband wears, be poisoned, for anything he knows: or the wholesome wine he drunk, even now, at the table –

KITELY.

{*Aside*} Now, God forbid: Oh me. Now, I remember,
My wife drunk to me, last: and changed the cup:
And bade me wear this cursed suit today.
See, if [98][heavn'] suffer murder undiscovered! –
I feel me ill; give me some mithridate,
Some mithridate and oil, good sister, fetch me;
Oh, I am sick at heart! I burn, I burn.
If you will save my life, go, fetch it me.

WELLBRED.

Oh, strange humour! My very breath has poisoned him.

BRIDGET.

Good brother, be content, what do you mean? The strength of these extreme conceits, will kill you.

DAME KITELY.

Beshrew your heart-blood, brother Wellbred, now;
For putting such a toy into his head.

WELLBRED.

Is a fit simile, a toy? Will he be poisoned with a simile? Brother Kitely, what a strange, and idle imagination is this? For shame, be wiser. Oh my soul, there's no such matter.

KITELY.

Am I not sick? How am I, then, not poisoned? Am I not poisoned? How am I, then, so sick?

DAME KITELY.

If you be sick, your own thoughts makes you sick.

WELLBRED.

His jealousy is the poison, he has taken.

{*Enter*} Brainworm. *He comes disguised like Justice Clement's*

---

[97] God!
[98] God

man, {Formal}.

BRAINWORM.

Master Kitely, my master, Justice Clement, salutes you; and desires to speak with you, with all possible speed.

KITELY.

No time, but now? When, I think, I am sick? Very sick! Well, I will wait upon his worship. Thomas, Cob! {*Aside*} I must seek them out, and set 'hem sentinels, till I return. – Thomas, Cob, Thomas.

{*Exit Kitely.*}

WELLBRED.

{*Takes Brainworm aside.*} This is perfectly rare, Brainworm! But how got'st thou this apparel, of the Justice's man?

BRAINWORM.

Marry sir, my proper fine pen-man, would needs bestow the grist o' me, at the [99][Windmill]; to hear some martial discourse; where so I marshalled him, that I made him[100] drunk, with admiration! And, because, too much heat was the cause of his distemper, I stripped him stark naked, as he lay along asleep, and borrowed his suit, to deliver this counterfeit message in, leaving a rusty armour, and an old brown bill to watch him, till my return: which shall be, when I ha' pawned his apparel, and spent the better part o' the money, perhaps.

WELLBRED.

Well, thou art a successful merry knave, Brainworm, his absence will be a good subject for more mirth. I pray thee, return to thy young master, and will him to meet me, and my sister Bridget, at the Tower instantly: for, here, tell him, the house is so stored with jealousy, there is no room for love, to stand upright in. We must get our fortunes committed to some larger prison, say; and, than the Tower, I know no better air: nor where the liberty of the house may do us more present service. Away.

{*Exit Brainworm.*}

{*Enter Kitely*}, *Cash* {*following*}.

KITELY.

Come hither, Thomas. Now, my secret's ripe,
And thou shalt have it: lay to both thine ears.
Hark, what I say to thee. I must go forth, Thomas.
Be careful of thy promise, keep good watch,
Note ever gallant, and observe him well,
That enters in my absence, to thy mistress:
If she would show him rooms, the jest is stale,
Follow 'hem, Thomas, or else hang on him,

And let him not go after; mark their looks;
Note, if she offer but to see his band,
Or any other amorous toy, about him;
But praise his leg; or foot; or if she say,
The day is hot, and bid him feel her hand,
How hot it is; Oh, that's a monstrous thing!
Note me all this, good Thomas, mark their sighs,
And, if they do but whisper, break 'hem off:
I'll bear thee out in it. Wilt thou do this?
Will thou be true, my Thomas?

CASH.   As truth's self, sir.

KITELY.

Why, I believe thee: where is Cob, now? Cob?

{*Exit Kitely.*}

DAME KITELY.

He's ever calling for Cob! I wonder, how he employs Cobs, so!

WELLBRED.

Indeed, sister, to ask how he employs Cob, is a necessary question for you, that are his wife, and a thing not very easy for you to be satisfied in: but this I'll assure you, Cob's wife is an excellent bawd, sister, and, oftentimes, your husband haunts her house, marry, to what end, I cannot altogether accuse him, imagine you what you think convenient. But, I have known, fair hides have foul hearts, ere now, sister.

DAME KITELY.

Never said you truer than that, brother, so much I can tell you for your learning. Thomas, fetch your cloak, and go with me, I'll after him presently.

{*Exit Cash.*}

I would to[101][fortune], I could take him there, i' faith. I'd return him his own, I warrant him.

{*Exit Dame Kitely.*}

WELLBRED.

[So, let 'hem go: this may make sport anon.] Now, my fair sister-in-law, that you knew, but how happy a thing it were to be fair, and beautiful?

BRIDGET.

That touches not me, brother.

---

[99] Mermaid
[100] *Insert:* monstrous
[101] Christ

WELLBRED.
That's true; that's even the fault of it: for, indeed, beauty stands a woman in no stead, unless it procure her touching. But, sister, whether it touch you, or no, it touches your beauties; and, I am sure, they will abide the touch; an' they do not, a plague of all ceruse, say I: and, it touches me too in part, though not in the – Well, there's a dear and respected friend of mine, sister, stands very strongly, and worthily affected toward you, and hath vowed to inflame whole bonfires of zeal, at his heart, in honour of your perfections. I have already engaged my promise to bring you, where you shall hear him confirm much more. Ned Kno'well is the man, sister. There's no exception against the party. You are ripe for a husband; and a minute's loss to such an occasion, is a great trespass in a wise beauty. What say you, sister? On my soul he loves you. Will you give him the meeting?

BRIDGET.
Faith, I had very little confidence in mine own constancy, brother, if I durst not meet a man: but this motion of yours, savours of an old night-adventurer's servant, a little too much, methinks.

WELLBRED.
What's that, sister?

BRIDGET.
Marry, of the squire.

WELLBRED.
No matter if it did, I would be such an one for my friend, but see! Who is returned to hinder us?

{Enter Kitely.}

KITELY.
What villainy is this? Called out on a false message? There was some plot! I was not sent for. Bridget, Where's your sister?

BRIDGET.   I think she be gone forth, sir.

KITELY.
How! Is my wife gone forth? Whither for God's sake?

BRIDGET.
She's gone abroad with Thomas.

KITELY.
Abroad with Thomas? Oh, that villain dors me.
He hath discovered all unto my wife!
Beast that I was, to trust him: whither, I pray you,
Went she?

BRIDGET.
I know not, sir.

WELLBRED.   I'll tell you, brother,
Whither I suspect she's gone.

KITELY.   Whither, good brother?

WELLBRED.
To Cob's house, I believe: but, keep my counsel.

KITELY.
I will, I will: to Cob's house? Doth she haunt Cob's?
She's gone a' purpose, now, to cuckold me,
With that lewd rascal, who, to win her favour,
Hath told her all.

{Exit.}

WELLBRED.   Come, he's once more gone.
Sister, let's lose no time; th' affair is worth it.

{Exeunt.}

Scene vii

{A Street. Enter} Matthew {and} Bobadill.

MATTHEW.
I wonder, Captain, what they will say of my going away? Ha?

BOBADILL.
Why, what should they say? But as of a discreet gentleman? Quick, wary, respectful of nature's fair lineaments: and that's all.

MATTHEW.
Why, so! But what can they say of your beating?

BOBADILL.
A rude part, a touch with soft wood, a kind of gross battery used, laid on strongly, borne most patiently: and that's all.

MATTHEW.
Ay, but, would any man have offered it in Venice? As you say?

BOBADILL.
Tut, I assure you, no: you shall have there your Nobilis, your Gentilezza, come in bravely upon your reverse, stand you close, stand you firm, stand you fair, save your retricato with his left leg, come to the asalto with the right, thrust with brave steel, defy your base wood! But, wherefore do I awake this

remembrance? I was fascinated, by [102][Jupiter]: fascinated: but I will be unwitched, and revenged, by law.

MATTHEW.
Do you hear? Is't not best to get a warrant, and have him arrested, and brought before Justice Clement.

BOBADILL.
It were not amiss, would we had it.

{Enter} Brainworm, {disguised as Formal}.

MATTHEW.
Why, here comes his man, let's speak to him.

BOBADILL.
Agreed, do you speak.

MATTHEW.
Save you, sir.

BRAINWORM.
With all my heart, sir.

MATTHEW.
Sir, there is one Downright, hath abused this gentleman, and myself, and we determine to make our amends by law; now, if you would do us the favour, to procure a warrant, to bring afore your master, you shall be well considered, I assure you, sir.

BRAINWORM.
Sir, you know my service is my living, such favours as these, gotten of my master, is his only preferment, and therefore, you must consider me, as I may make benefit of my place.

MATTHEW.
How is that, sir?

BRAINWORM.
Faith sir, the thing is extraordinary, and the gentleman may be, of great account: yet, be what he will, if you will lay me down [103][a brace of angels], in my hand, you shall have it, otherwise not.

MATTHEW.
How shall we do? Captain? He asks [104][a brace of angels], you have no money?

BOBADILL.
Not a cross, by [105][fortune].

MATTHEW.
Nor I, as I am a gentleman, but twopence, left of my two shillings in the morning for wine, and radish: let's find him some pawn.

BOBADILL.
Pawn? We have none to the value of his demand.

MATTHEW.
Oh, yes, I'll pawn this jewel in my ear, and you may pawn your silk stockings, and pull up your boots, they will ne'er be missed: it must be done, now.

BOBADILL.
Well, an' there be no remedy: I'll step aside, and pull 'hem off.

MATTHEW.
Do you hear, sir? We have no store of money at this time, but you shall have good pawns: look you, sir, this jewel, and that gentleman's silk stockings, because we would have it dispatched, ere we went to our chambers.

BRAINWORM.
I am content, sir; I will get you the warrant presently, what's his name, say you? Downright?

MATTHEW.
Ay, ay, George Downright.

BRAINWORM.
What manner of man is he?

MATTHEW.
A tall big man, sir; he goes in a cloak, most commonly, of silk russet, laid about with russet lace.

BRAINWORM.
'Tis very good, sir.

MATTHEW.
Here sir, here's my jewel.

BOBADILL.
And, here, are stockings.

BRAINWORM.
Well, gentleman, I'll procure you this warrant presently, but, who will you have to serve it?

MATTHEW.
That's true, Captain: that must be considered.

BOBADILL.
Body o' me, I know not! 'Tis service of danger!

---

[102] Jesu
[103] five crowns
[104] five crowns
[105] Jesu

BRAINWORM.

Why, you were best get one o' the varlets o' the city, a sergeant.
I'll appoint you one, if you please.

MATTHEW.

Will you, sir? Why, we can wish no better.

BOBADILL.

We'll leave it to you, sir.

{*Exeunt Bobadill and Matthew.*}

BRAINWORM.

This is rare! Now, will I go pawn this cloak of the Justice's
man's, at the brokers, for a varlet's suit, and be the varlet
myself; and get either more pawns, or more money of
Downright, for the arrest.

{*Exit.*}

Scene viii

{*The Lane before Cob's House. Enter*} Kno'well.

KNO'WELL.

Oh, here it is, I am glad: I have found it now. Ho! Who is
within, here?

{*Knocks at Cob's door.*}

TIB.

{*From within*} I am within sir, what's your pleasure?

KNO'WELL.

To know, who is within, besides yourself.

TIB.

Why, sir, you are no constable, I hope?

KNO'WELL.

Oh! Fear you the constable? Then, I doubt not,
You have some guests within, deserve that fear,
I'll fetch him straight.

{*Tib opens.*}

TIB.   O' God's name, sir.

KNO'WELL.

Go to. Come, tell me, is not young Kno'well, here?

TIB.

Young Kno'well? I know none such, sir, o' mine honesty!

KNO'WELL.

Your honesty? Dame, it flies too lightly from you:
There is no way, but, fetch the constable.

TIB.

The constable? The man is mad, I think.

{*Exit Tib.*}

{*Enter*} Dame Kitely {*and*} Cash.

CASH.

Ho, who keeps house, here?

KNO'WELL.

Oh, this is the female copesmate of my son.
Now shall I meet him straight.

DAME KITELY.   Knock, Thomas, hard.

CASH.

Ho, good wife?

{*Tib opens door a crack.*}

TIB.   Why, what's the matter with you?

DAME KITELY.

Why, woman, grieves it you to ope' your door?
Belike, you get something, to keep it shut.

TIB.

What mean these questions, 'pray ye?

DAME KITELY.

So strange you make it? Is not my husband, here?

KNO'WELL.

Her husband!

DAME KITELY.   My tried husband, Master Kitely.

TIB.

I hope, he needs not to be tried, here.

DAME KITELY.

No, dame: he does it not for need, but pleasure.

TIB.

Neither for need, nor pleasure, is he here.

KNO'WELL.

This is but a device, to baulk me withal.

{*Enter*} Kitely.

Soft, who is this? 'Tis not my son, disguised?

DAME KITELY.

(*She spies her husband come: and runs to him.*)
Oh, sir, have I forestalled your honest market?
Found your close walks? You stand amazed, now, do you?
I' faith, I am glad, I have smoked you yet at last!
Where is your jewel trow? In: come, let's see her –
Fetch forth your housewife, dame – if she be fairer,
In any honest judgement, than myself,
I'll be content with it: but, she is change,
She feeds you fat, she soothes your appetite,
And you are well? Your wife, an honest woman,
Is meat twice sod to you, sir? Oh, you treachour!

KNO'WELL.

She cannot counterfeit thus plausibly.

KITELY.

Out on thy more than strumpet's impudence!
Steal'st thou thus to thy haunts? And, have I taken
They bawd, and thee, and thy companion,

(*Pointing to Old Kno'well.*)

This hoary-headed lecher, this old goat,
Close at your villainy, and would'st thou 'scuse it,
With this stale harlot's hest, accusing me?
(*To him.*) Oh, old incontinent, does not thou shame,
When all thy powers in chastity is spent,
To have a mind so hot? And to entice,
And feed th' enticements of a lustful woman?

DAME KITELY.

Out, I defy thee, I, dissembling wretch!

KITELY.

Defy me, strumpet. {*Indicates Cash.*} Ask thy pandar, here,
Can he deny it? Or that wicked elder?

KNO'WELL.

Why, hear you, sir.

KITELY.   Tut, tut, tut: never speak.
Thy guilty conscience will discover thee.

KNO'WELL.

What lunacy is this, that haunts this man?

106

[KITELY.

Well, good wife B – A –' – D, Cob's wife; and you,]
That make your husband such a hoddy-doddy;
And you, young apple-squire; and old cuckold-maker;

I'll ha, you every one before a justice:
Nay, you shall answer it, I charge you go.

KNO'WELL.

Marry, with all my heart, sir: I go willingly.
Though I do taste this as a trick, put on me,
To punish my impertinent search; and justly:
And half forgive my son, for the device.

KITELY.

Come, will you go?

DAME KITELY.   Go? To thy shame, believe it.

{*Enter*} Cob.

COB.

Why, what's the matter, here? What's here to do?

KITELY.

Oh, Cob, art thou come? I have been abused,
And i' thy house. Never was man so, wronged!

COB.

'Slid, in my house? My Master Kitely? Who wrongs you in my
house?

KITELY.

Marry, young lust in old; and old in young, here:
Thy wife's their bawd, here have I taken 'hem.

---

[106] *Insert:* {*Enter Downright.*}

DOWNRIGHT.
    Oh, sister, did you see my cloak?
DAME KITELY.
    Not I, I see none.
DOWNRIGHT.
    God's life, I have lost it then. Saw you Bridget?
KITELY.
    Bridget? Is she not at home?
DOWNRIGHT.
    No, she is gone abroad, and nobody can tell me of it at
    home.
                                        {*Exit.*}
KITELY.
    O heaven! abroad? What light! a harlot too!
    Why? Why? Hark you, hath she, hath she not a brother?
    A brother's house to keep, to look unto?
    But she must fling abroad. My wife hath spoil'd her.
    She takes right after her, she does, she does.
    Well, goody B – A –' –D, Cob's wife and you,

COB.

How? Bawd? Is my house come to that? Am I preferred thither? (*He falls upon his wife and beats her.*) Did I charge you to keep your doors shut, Is'bel? And do you let 'hem open for all comers?

KNO'WELL.

Friend, know some cause, before thou beat'st thy wife,
This's madness, in thee.

COB.   Why? Is there no cause?

KITELY.

Yes, I'll show cause before the Justice, Cob:
Come, let her go with me.

COB.   Nay, she shall go.

TIB.

Nay, I will go. I'll see, an' you may be allowed to make a bundle o' hemp, o' your right and lawful wife thus, at every cuckoldly knave's pleasure[107] Why do you not go?

KITELY.

A bitter quean. Come, we'll ha' you tamed.

{*Exeunt.*}

Scene ix

{*A Street. Enter*} Brainworm {*disguised as a city-sergeant.*}

BRAINWORM.

Well, of all my disguises, yet, now am I most like myself: being in this sergeant's gown. [A man of my present profession, never counterfeits, till he lays hold upon a debtor, and says, he rests him, for then he brings him to all manner of unrest.] A kind of little kings we are, bearing the diminutive of a mace, made like a young artichoke, that always carries pepper and salt, in itself. Well, I know not what danger I undergo, by this exploit, pray [108][heaven], I come well off.

{*Enter*} Matthew {*and*} Bobadill.

MATTHEW.

See, I think, yonder is the varlet, by his gown.

BOBADILL.

Let's go, in quest of him.

MATTHEW.

[109]Save you, friend, are you not here, by appointment of Justice

Clement's man?

BRAINWORM.

Yes, an't please you, sir: he told me two gentlemen had willed him to procure a warrant from his master, which I have about me, to be served on one Downright.

MATTHEW.

It is honestly done of you both; and see, where the party comes, you must arrest: serve it upon him, quickly, afore he be aware –

BOBADILL.

Bear back, Master Matthew.

{*Enter*} Stephen {*in Downright's cloak.*}

BRAINWORM.

Master Downright, I arrest you, i' the Queen's name, and must carry you afore a justice, by virtue of this warrant.

STEPHEN.

Me, friend? I am no Downright, I, I am Master Stephen, you do not well, [110][to arrest me, I tell you, truly: I am in nobody's bonds, nor books,] I, would you should know it. A plague[111] on you heartily, for making me thus fraid afore my time.

BRAINWORM.

Why, now are you deceived, gentlemen?

BOBADILL.

He wears such a cloak, and that deceived us: but see, here a comes, indeed! This is he, officer.

{*Enter*} Downright.

DOWNRIGHT.

Why, how now, signior gull! Are you turned filcher of late? Come, deliver my cloak.

STEPHEN.

Your cloak, sir? I bought it, even now, in open market.

BRAINWORM.

Master Downright, I have a warrant I must serve upon you, procured by these two gentlemen.

---

[107] *Insert:* The devil and the pox take you all for me.
[108] God
[109] *Insert:* God
[110] *Insert:* by God's lid, to arrest me. I tell you, truly: I am not in your master's books,
[111] *Insert:* of God

DOWNRIGHT.
These gentlemen? These rascals! {*Raises his cudgel.*}

BRAINWORM.
Keep the peace, I charge you, in her Majesty's name.

DOWNRIGHT.
I obey thee. What must I do, officer?

BRAINWORM.
Go before Master Justice Clement, to answer what they can object against you, sir. I will use your kindly, sir.

112[MATTHEW.
Come, let's before, and make the Justice, Captain –

BOBADILL.
The varlet's a tall man! Afore heaven!]

{*Exeunt Matthew and Bobadill.*}

STEPHEN.
Sir, I bought it, and I'll keep it.

DOWNRIGHT.
You will.

STEPHEN.
Ay, that I will.

DOWNRIGHT.
Officer, there's thy fee, arrest him.

BRAINWORM.
Master Stephen, I must arrest you.

STEPHEN.
Arrest me, I scorn it. There, take your cloak, I'll none on't.

DOWNRIGHT.
Nay, that shall not serve your turn, now, sir. Officer, I'll go with thee, to the Justice's: bring him along.

STEPHEN.
Why, is not here your cloak? What would you have?

DOWNRIGHT.
I'll ha' you answer it, sir.

BRAINWORM.
Sir, I'll take your word; and this gentleman's, too: for his appearance.

DOWNRIGHT.
I'll ha' no words taken. Bring him along.

BRAINWORM.
Sir, I may choose, to do that: I may take bail.

DOWNRIGHT.
'Tis true, you may take bail, and choose; at another time: but you shall not, now, varlet. Bring him along, or I'll swinge you.

{*Downright raises cudgel.*}

BRAINWORM.
Sir, I pity the gentleman's case. Here's your money again.

DOWNRIGHT.
113['Sdeins], tell not me of my money, bring him away, I say.

BRAINWORM.
I warrant you he will go with you of himself, sir.

DOWNRIGHT.
Yet more ado?

BRAINWORM.
{*Aside*} I have made a fair mash114[on't].

STEPHEN.
Must I go?

BRAINWORM.
I know no remedy, Master Stephen.

DOWNRIGHT.
Come along, afore me, here. I do not love your hanging look behind.

STEPHEN.
Why sir. I hope you cannot hang me for it. Can he, fellow?

BRAINWORM.
I think not, sir. It is but a whipping matter, sure.

STEPHEN.
Why, then, let him do his worse, I am resolute.

{*Exeunt.*}

---

112 MATTHEW.
We'll be even with you sir. Come, Captain Bobadill, let's before and prepare the Justice. Varlet, look to him.
BOBADILL.
The varlet's a tall man, by Jesu!

(*Exeunt Matthew and Bobadill.*)

113 God's bread,
114 of it

ACT FIVE

Scene i

{Coleman Street. A Hall in Justice Clement's House. Enter} Clement, Kno'well, Kitely, Dame Kitely, Tib, Cash, Cob {and} Servants.

CLEMENT.
Nay, but stay, stay, give me leave: my chair, sirrah. You, Master Kno'well, say you went thither to meet your son.

KNO'WELL.
Ay, sir.

CLEMENT.
But, who directed you, thither?

KNO'WELL.
That did mine own man, sir.

CLEMENT.
Where is he?

KNO'WELL.
Nay, I know not, now; I left him with your clerk: and appointed him, to stay here for me.

CLEMENT.
My clerk? About what time, was this?

KNO'WELL.
Marry, between one and two, as I take it.

CLEMENT.
And, what time came my man with the false message to you, Master Kitely?

KITELY.
After two, sir.

CLEMENT.
Very good: but, Mistress Kitely, how that you were at Cob's? Ha?

DAME KITELY.
An' please you, sir, I'll tell you: my brother, Wellbred, told me, that Cob's house, was a suspected place –

CLEMENT.
So it appears, methinks: but, on.

DAME KITELY.
And that my husband used thither, daily.

CLEMENT.
No matter, so he used himself well, mistress.

DAME KITELY.
True sir, but you now, what grows, by such haunts, oftentimes.

CLEMENT.
I see, rank fruits of a jealous brain, Mistress Kitely: but, did you find your husband there, in that case, as you suspected?

KITELY.
I found her there, sir.

CLEMENT.
Did you so? That alters the case. Who gave you knowledge, of your wife's being there.

KITELY.
Marry, that did my brother Wellbred.

CLEMENT.
How? Wellbred first tell her? Then tell you, after? Where is Wellbred?

KITELY.
Gone with my sister, sir, I know not whither.

CLEMENT.
Why, this is a mere trick, a device; you are gulled in this most grossly, all! Alas, poor wench, wert thou beaten for this?

TIB.
Yes, most pitifully, and't please you.

COB.
And worthily, I hope: if it shall prove so.

CLEMENT.
Ay, that's like, and a piece of a sentence.

{Enter a Servant.}

How now, sir? What's the matter?

SERVANT.
Sir, there's a gentleman, i' the court without, desires to speak with your worship.

CLEMENT.
A gentleman? What's he?

SERVANT.
A soldier, sir, he says.

CLEMENT.
A soldier? Take down my armour, my sword, quickly: a soldier speak with me! Why, when knaves?

(*He arms himself.*)

Come on, come on, hold my cap there, so; give me my gorget, my sword: stand by, I will end your matters, anon – Let the soldier enter.

(*{Enter} Bobadill {and} Matthew. {Exit Servant}*)

Now, sir what ha' you to say to me?

BOBADILL.
By your worship's favour –

CLEMENT.
Nay, keep out, sir, I know not your pretence, you send me word, sir, you are a soldier: why, sir, you shall be answered, here, here be them have been amongst soldiers. Sir, your pleasure.

BOBADILL.
Faith, sir, so it is, this gentleman, and myself, have been most uncivilly wronged, and beaten, by one Downright, a coarse fellow, about the town, here, and for mine own part, I protest, being a man, in no sort, given to this filthy humour of quarrelling, he hath assaulted me in the way of my peace; despoiled me of mine honour; disarmed me of my weapons; and rudely, laid me along, in the open streets: when, I not so much as once offered to resist him.

CLEMENT.
Oh, God's precious! Is this the soldier? Here, take my armour off quickly, 'twill make him swoon, I fear; he is not fit to look on't, that will put up a blow.

MATTHEW.
An't please your worship, he was bound to the peace.

CLEMENT.
Why, and he were, sir, his hands were not bound, were they?

{*Enter Servant*}

SERVANT.
There's one of the varlets of the city, sir, has brought two gentlemen, here, one, upon your worship's warrant.

CLEMENT.
My warrant?

SERVANT.
Yes, sir. The officer says, procured by these two.

CLEMENT.
Bid him, come in.

{*Exit Servant.*}

Set by this picture.

(*{Enter} Downright, Stephen {and} Brainworm {disguised as a city sergeant.}*)

What, Master Downright! Are you brought at Master Freshwater's suit, here?

DOWNRIGHT.
I' faith, sir. And here's another brought at my suit.

CLEMENT.
What are you, sir?

STEPHEN.
A gentleman, sir. Oh, uncle!

CLEMENT.
Uncle? Who? Master Kno'well?

KNO'WELL.
Ay, sir! This is a wise kinsman of mine.

STEPHEN.
God's my witness, uncle, I am wronged here monstrously, he charges me with stealing of his cloak, and would I might never stir, if I did not find it in the street, by chance.

DOWNRIGHT.
Oh, did you find it, now? You said, you bought it, erewhile.

STEPHEN.
And, you said, I stole it; nay, now my uncle is here, I'll do well enough, with you.

CLEMENT.
Well, let this breathe a while; you, that have cause to complain, there, stand forth: had you my warrant for this gentleman's apprehension?

BOBADILL.
Ay, an't please your worship.

CLEMENT.
Nay, do not speak in passion so: where had you it?

BOBADILL.
Of your clerk, sir.

CLEMENT.
That's well! An' my clerk can make warrants, and my hand not

at 'hem! Where is the warrant? Officer, have you it?

BRAINWORM.

No, sir, your worship's man, Master Formal, bid me do it, for these gentlemen, and he would be my discharge.

CLEMENT.

Why, Master Downright, are you such a novice, to be served, and never see the warrant?

DOWNRIGHT.

Sir. He did not serve it on me.

CLEMENT.

No? How then?

DOWNRIGHT.

Marry, sir, he came to me, and said, he must serve it, and he would use me kindly, and so –

CLEMENT.

Oh, God's pity, was it so, sir? He must serve it? Give me my long-sword there, [and help me off;] so. Come on, sir varlet, I must cut off your legs, sirrah:

({*Brainworm kneels.*} *He flourishes over him with his long-sword.*)

nay, stand up, I'll use you kindly; I must cut off your legs, I say.

BRAINWORM.

{*Kneeling again.*} Oh, good sir, I beseech you; nay, good Master Justice.

CLEMENT.

I must do it; there is no remedy. I *must* cut off your legs, sirrah, I must cut off your ears, you rascal, I must do it; I must cut off your nose, I must cut off your head.

BRAINWORM.

Oh, good your worship.

CLEMENT.

Well, rise, how dost thou do, now? Dost thou feel thyself well? Hast thou no harm?

BRAINWORM.

No, I thank your good worship, sir.

CLEMENT.

Why, so? I said, I must cut off thy legs, and I must cut off thy arms, and I must cut off thy head; but, I did not do it: so, you said, you must serve this gentleman, with my warrant, but, you did not serve him. You knave, you slave, you rogue, do you say you must? Sirrah, away with him, to the jail, I'll teach you a trick, for your *must*, sir.

BRAINWORM.

Good sir, I beseech you, be good to me.

CLEMENT.

Tell him he shall to the jail, away with him, I say.

BRAINWORM.

Nay, sir, if you will commit me, it shall be for committing more than this: I will not lose, by my travail, any grain of my fame certain.

{*Brainworm throws off his disguise.*}

CLEMENT.

How is this!

KNO'WELL.

My man, Brainworm!

STEPHEN.

Oh yes, uncle. Brainworm has been with my cousin Edward, and I, all this day.

CLEMENT.

I told you all, there was some device!

BRAINWORM.

Nay, excellent Justice, since I have laid myself thus open to you; now, stand strong for me: both with your sword, and your balance.

CLEMENT.

Body o' me, a merry knave! Give me a bowl of sack: if he belongs to you, Master Kno'well, I bespeak your patience.

BRAINWORM.

That is it, I have most need of. Sir, if you'll pardon me, only; I'll glory in all the rest, of my exploits.

KNO'WELL.

Sir, you know, I love not to have my favours come hard, from me. You have your pardon: though I suspect you shrewdly for being of counsel with my son, against me.

BRAINWORM.

Yes, faith, I have, sir; though you retained me doubly this morning, for yourself: first, as Brainworm; after, as Fitzsword. I was your reformed soldier, sir. 'Twas I sent you to Cob's, upon the errand, without end.

KNO'WELL.

Is it possible! Or that thou should'st disguise thy language so, as I should not know thee?

BRAINWORM.

Oh, sir, this has been the day of my metamorphosis! It is not that shape alone, that I have run through, today. I brought this gentleman, Master Kitely, a message too, in the form of Master Justice's man, here, to draw him out o' the way, as well as your worship: while Master Wellbred might make a conveyance of Mistress Bridget, to my young master.

KITELY.

How! My sister stol'n away?

KNO'WELL.

My son is not married, I hope!

BRAINWORM.

Faith, sir, they are both as sure as love, a priest, and three thousand pound, which is her portion, can make 'hem: and by this time are ready to bespeak their wedding supper at the Windmill, except some friend, here, prevent 'hem, and invite 'hem home.

CLEMENT.

Marry, that will I. I thank thee, for putting me in mind on't. Sirrah, go you, and fetch 'hem hither, upon my warrant. Neither's friends have cause to be sorry, if I know the young couple, aright. Here, I drink to thee, for thy good news. But, I pray thee, what has thou done with my man Formal?

BRAINWORM.

Faith, sir, after some ceremony past, as making him drunk, first with story, and then with wine – but all in kindness – and stripping him to his shirt: I left him in that cool vain, departed, sold your worship's warrant to these two, pawned his livery for that varlet's gown, to serve it in; and thus have brought myself, by my activity, to your worship's consideration.

CLEMENT.

And I will consider thee, in another cup of sack. Here's to thee, which having drunk off, this is my sentence. Pledge me. Thou hast done, or assisted to nothing, in my judgement, but deserves to be pardoned for the wit o' the offence. If thy master, or any man, here, be angry with thee, I shall suspect his ingine, while I know him for't. How now? What noise is that?

{Enter Servant.}

SERVANT.

Sir, it is Roger coming home.

CLEMENT.

Bring him in, bring him in.

{Enter} Formal {in a suit of armour.}

What! Drunk in arms, against me? Your reason, your reason for this.

FORMAL.

I beseech your worship to pardon me; I happened into ill company by chance, that cast me into a sleep, and stripped me of all my clothes –

CLEMENT.

Well, tell him, I am Justice Clement, and do pardon him: but, what is this to your armour! What may that signify?

FORMAL.

And't please you, sir, it hung up i' the room, where I was stripped; and I borrowed it of one o' the drawers, to come home in, because I was loath, to do penance through the street, i' my shirt.

CLEMENT.

Well, stand by a while.

{Enter} Ed. Kno'well, Wellbred, {and} Bridget.

Who be these? Oh, the young company, welcome, welcome. Gi' you joy. Nay, Mistress Bridget, blush not; you are not so fresh a bride, but the news of it is come hither afore you. Master Bridegroom, I ha' made your peace, give me your hand: so will I for all the rest, ere you forsake my roof.

ED. KNO'WELL.

We are the more bound to your humanity, sir.

CLEMENT.

Only these two, have so little of man in 'hem, they are no part of my care.

WELLBRED.

Yes, sir, let me pray you for this gentleman, he belongs, to my sister, the bride.

CLEMENT.

In what place, sir?

WELLBRED.

Of her delight, sir, below the stairs, and in public: her *poet*, sir.

CLEMENT.

A *poet*? I will challenge him myself, presently, at *extempore*.
    Mount up thy Phlegon muse, and testify,
        How Saturn, sitting in an ebon cloud,
    Disrobed his podex white as ivory,
        And, through the welkin, thundered all aloud.

WELLBRED.

He is not for *extempore*, sir. He is all for the pocket-muse, please you command a sight of it.

CLEMENT.
Yes, yes, search him for a taste of his vein.

{*They search Matthew's pockets.*}

WELLBRED.
You must not deny the Queen's Justice, sir, under a writ o' rebellion.

CLEMENT.
What! All this verse? Body o' me, he carries a whole realm, a commonwealth of paper, in's hose! Let's see some of his subjects!
Unto the boundless Ocean of thy face,
Runs this poor river charged with streams of eyes.
How? This is stol'n.

115[ED. KNO'WELL.
A parody! A parody! With a kind of miraculous gift, to make it absurder than it was.

CLEMENT.
Is all the rest, of this batch? Bring me a torch; lay it] together, and give fire. Cleanse the air. Here was enough to have infected, the whole city, if it had not been taken in time! See, see, how our *Poet's* glory shines! Brighter and brighter! Still it increases! Oh, now, it's at the highest: and, now, it declines as fast. You may see. *Sic transit gloria mundi.*

KNO'WELL.
There's an emblem for you, son, and your studies!

CLEMENT.
Nay, [no speech, or act of mine be drawn against such, as profess it worthily.] They are not born every year, as an alderman. There goes more to the making of a good poet, than a sheriff, Master Kitely. You look upon me! Though, I live i' the city here, amongst you, I will do more reverence, to him, when

---

115

MATTHEW.
No, sir, I translated that out of a book, called Delia.
CLEMENT.
Oh, but I would see some of your own, some of your own.
MATTHEW.
Sir, here's the beginning of a sonnet I made to my mistress.
CLEMENT.
That, that: who? To Madonna Bridget? Is she your mistress?

WELLBRED.
It pleaseth him to call her so, sir.
CLEMENT.
'In summer time, when Phoebus' golden rays'. You translated this too, did you not?
WELLBRED.
No, this is invention; he found it in a ballad.
MATTHEW.
Faith sir, I had most of the conceit of it out of a ballad indeed.
CLEMENT.
Conceit! Fetch me a couple of torches, sirrah, I may see the conceit: quickly! It's very dark!
DOWNRIGHT {*reading*}
Call you this poetry?
ED. KNO'WELL.
Poetry? Nay, then, call blasphemy, religion;
Call devils, angels; and sin, piety:
Let all things be preposterously transchanged.
KNO'WELL.
Why, how now, son! What are you startled now?
Hath the brize prick'd you, ha? Go to; you see
How abjectly your poetry is ranked in general opinion.
ED. KNO'WELL.
Opinion, O God, let gross opinion
Sink and be damn'd as deep as Barathrum,
Indeed, if you will look on Poetry
As she appears in many, poor and lame,
Patch'd up in remnants and old worn rags,
Half starved for want of her peculiar food:
Sacred invention, then I must confirm
Both your conceit and censure of her merit;
But view her in her glorious ornaments
Attired in the majesty of art,
Oh, then how proud a presence doth she bear.
Nor is it any blemish to her fame,
That such lean, ignorant, and blasted wits,
Such brainless gulls should utter their stol'n wares
With such applauses in our vulgar ears:
Or that their slubber'd lines have current pass
From the fat judgements of the multitude,
But that this barren and infected age
Should set no difference 'twist these empty spirits
And a true poet: than which reverend name
Nothing can more adorn humanity.
{*Enter Servants with torches.*}
CLEMENT.
Give me thy torch; come, lay this stuff

I meet him, than I will to the [116][major], out of his year. [But, these paper-pedlars! These ink dabblers! They cannot expect reprehension, or reproach. They have it with the fact.

ED. KNO'WELL.

Sir, you have saved me the labour of a defence.]

CLEMENT.

It shall be discourse for supper; between your father and me, if he dare undertake me. But[117], to dispatch away these, you sign o' the soldier, and picture o' the poet – [118][but, both so false, I will not ha' you hanged out at my door till midnight – while we are at supper, you two shall penitently fast it in my court, without; and, if you will, you may pray there, that we may be so merry within, as to forgive, or forget you, when we come out. Here's a third, because, we tender your safety, shall watch you, he is provided for the purpose. Look to your charge, sir.]

STEPHEN.

And what shall I do?

CLEMENT.

Oh! I had lost a sheep, an he had not bleated! Why, sir, you shall give Master Downright his cloak: and I will entreat him to take it. A trencher, and a napkin, you shall have, i' the buttery, and keep Cob, and his wife company, here; whom, I will entreat first to be reconciled; and you to endeavour with your wit, to keep 'hem so.

STEPHEN.

I'll do my best.

COB.

Why, now I see thou art honest, Tib, I receive thee as my dear, and mortal wife, again.

TIB.

And, I you, as my loving, and obedient husband.

CLEMENT.

Good complement! It will be their bridal night, too. They are married anew. Come, I conjure the rest, to put off all discontent. You, Master Downright, your anger; you, Master Kno'well, your cares; Master Kitely, and his wife, their jealousy.

[119]['For, I must tell you both, while that is fed,
Horns i' the mind are worse than o' the head'.]

KITELY.

Sir, thus they go from me, kiss me, sweetheart.

'See what a drove of horns fly, in the air,
Winged with my cleansed, and my credulous breath!
Watch 'hem, suspicious eyes, watch, where they fall.

See, see! On heads, that think they've none at all!
Oh, what a plenteous world of this, will come!
When air rains horns, all may be sure of some'.]

I ha' learned so much verse out of a jealous man's part, in a play.

CLEMENT.

'Tis well, 'tis well! This night we'll dedicate to friendship, love, and laughter. Master bridegroom, take your bride, and lead; every one, a fellow. Here is my mistress – Brainworm! To whom all my addresses of courtship shall have their reference. Whose adventures, this day, when our grandchildren shall hear to be made a fable, I doubt not, but it shall find both spectators, and applause.

The end.

---

[116] mayor

[117] *Insert:* now

[118] CLEMENT.

stand forth, and lend me your large ears – while we are at supper, you two shall penitently fast it in my court without, and both together sing some ballad of repentance very piteously, which you shall make to the tune of 'Who list to lead and a soldier's life', and if you will, you may pray there, that we may be so merry within, as to forgive, or forget you, when we come out. Here's a third, because, we tender your safety, shall watch you. He is provided for the purpose. Look to your charge, sir.

BOBADILL.

Well, I am arm'd in soul against the worst of fortune.

MATTHEW.

Faith, so should I be, an I had slept on it.

FORMAL.

I am arm'd too, but I am not like to sleep on it.

{*Exeunt Bobadill, Matthew and Formal.*}

[119] *Insert:* DOWNRIGHT.

Brother Wellbred, I am loth to kindle fresh coals, but an you had come in my walk within these two hours I had given you that you should not have clawed off again in haste, by Jesus, I had done it, I am the arrant'st rogue that ever breathed else. But now, beshrew my heart if I bear you any malice in the earth.

WELLBRED.

Faith, I did it but to hold up a jest, and help our sister Bridget to a husband. But brother Kitely, and sister, you have a spice of the jealous yet, both of you. Come do not dwell upon your anger so much.

DAME KITELY.

Brother, had he no haunt thither, in good faith?

WELLBRED.

No, upon my soul.

DAME KITELY.

Nay then, sweetheart: nay, I pray thee, be not angry, good faith, I'll never suspect thee any more. Nay, kiss me, sweet muss.

KITELY.

Tell me, wife, do you not play the woman with me?

DAME KITELY.

What's that, sweetheart?

KITELY.

Dissemble.

DAME KITELY.

Dissemble?

KITELY.

Nay, do not turn away: but say i'faith was it not a match appointed 'twixt this old gentleman and you?

DAME KITELY.

A match?

KITELY.

Nay, if it were not, I do not care. Do not weep, I pray thee, sweetheart. Nay, so now. By Jesus, I am not jealous, but resolved I have the faithful'st wife in London. Kiss me sweetheart.

> *Wretched and foolish Jealousie,*
> *How cam'st thou thus to enter me?*
> > *I ne'er was of thy kind;*
> *Nor have I yet the narrow mind*
> > *To vent that poor desire,*
> *That others should not warm them at my fire,*
> > *I wish the Sun should shine*
> *On all mens Fruit, and flowers as well as mine.*
>
> *But under the disguise of love,*
> *Thou sai'st, thou only came to prove*
> > *What my affections were.*
> *Think'st thou that love is help'd by fear?*
> > *Goe, get thee quickly forth,*
> *Loves sicknesse, and his noted want of worth,*
> > *Seeke doubting Men to please,*
> *I ne'er will owe my health to a disease.*